SUDDENLY
THEY'RE

13

or the art of hugging a cactus

A Parent's Survival Guide
for the Adolescent Years

David and Claudia Arp

An updated and revised edition of *Almost 13*

D0359366

ZONDERVAN™

GRAND RAPIDS, MICHIGAN 49530

ZONDERVAN™

Suddenly They're 13
Copyright © 1999 by Dave and Claudia Arp
An updated and revised edition of *Almost 13*

Requests for information should be addressed to:

Zondervan, *Grand Rapids, Michigan 49530*

Library of Congress Cataloging-in-Publication Data

Arp, Dave.
    Suddenly they're 13: or the art of hugging a cactus / David and Claudia Arp.
    p. cm.
    Rev. ed. of Almost 13. ©1986.
    ISBN 0-310-22788-7
    1. Teenagers—United States. 2. Parent and Teenager—United States. 3.
Adolescent psychology—United States. 4. Parenting—Religious aspects—
Christianity. I. Arp, Claudia. II. Arp, Dave. Almost 13. III. Title. IV. Title:
Suddenly they're thirteen.
HQ796.A728 1999
305.235—dc21   98-18213

Published in association with Alive Communications, Inc., 7680 Goddard Street,
Suite 200, Colorado Springs, CO 80920.

Throughout this book, names and details have been changed to protect their
privacy.

This book is a resource for family enrichment and not a substitute for needed
professional help.

Illustrations by Steve Björkman. Used by permission.

Interior design by Sherri L. Hoffman

Printed in the United States of America

04 05 /❖ DC/ 10 9 8 7

David and Claudia Arp's book *Suddenly They're 13* is a lifesaver for parents whose kids are entering the adolescent years. With a refreshing blend of vulnerability, practicality, and humor, the Arps offer valuable strategies and much encouragement to help readers steer their kids in a positive direction and build a lasting relationship with them during the teenage years.

> Cheri Fuller, Author of *When Mothers Pray*
> and *Through the Learning Glass*

Suddenly They're 13 is an amazing source of encouragement to parents who are trying desperately to connect in positive ways with their teenagers.

> Ken R. Canfield, Ph.D., Founder and President
> The National Center for Fathering

A straight-up, honest, parent-to-parent guide to keeping your heart connected with your teen.

> Dr. Timothy Clinton, President
> American Association of Christian Counselors

A creative and practical guide for parents of preteens. Instead of dreading these years, this book will help you enjoy them. Required reading for parents of any school-age child.

> Linda Dillow, Author of *Calm My Anxious Heart*

Suddenly They're 13 is one of the most readable, usable, and reliable self-study pre-and midteen manuals on the market. For the parent who is serious about growing responsible and caring adults, this book could well serve as a family life preserver.

> Howard and Jeanne Hendricks
> Authors of *Living by the Book* and *Women of Honor*

An excellent resource for parents of preteens and teens. The authors' personal experiences and creative perspective make this a valuable tool for all who work with children.

> Dr. D. Ross Campbell, Author of *How to Really Love Your Teenager*
> and *How to Really Love Your Child*

Suddenly They're 13 is very practical, with exercises, real-life stories, illustrations, and suggested activities. Any parent using this book as a guide would better manage this critical task in family life.

> Dr. Vera Mace, Co-founder of the American
> Association of Marriage and Family Therapy

*To all the parents in
PEP Groups for Parents of Teens
and those in our other parenting groups
who over the years have encouraged
other parents of adolescents*

CONTENTS

ACKNOWLEDGMENTS

We gratefully acknowledge the contributions of the following people:

—All the parents who have participated in our parenting groups over the years including Mom's & Dad's Support Groups, MOM's Support Group and PEP Groups for Parents of Teens for your great feedback and help in making this book much broader than just a "one-family" experience.

— Our excellent support team at Zondervan including our editors Sandy Vander Zicht and Mary McNeil for their friendship and editing expertise, Jody Langley for her great art that makes our books look like so much fun, John Topliff and his fine marketing team for helping to get our books to those who need them, Joyce Ondersma and Jackie Aldridge for being special friends and for taking such good care of us, and Scott Bolinder, our publisher and personal encourager, for continuing to believe in us and helping us help others.

—Steve Björkman for partnering with us over the years in encouraging families and for letting us use his wonderful illustrations once again.

—Our friends over the years who encouraged us to keep on encouraging parents of adolescents, including John and Jane Bell, Bill and Kathy Clarke, Paul and Phyllis Stanley, Jody and Linda Dillow, Clark and Ann Peddicord, Susan Farris, Cynthia Smith, and Mel Amerine.

—Our Marriage Alive team for all your support and help including Rich and Pam Batten, Autumn Whiteman, Jonathan Arp, and Laurie Clark.

—Our literary agent, Greg Johnson of Alive Communications, for being our advocate.

—Our three sons, now parents themselves, who taught us more than we probably ever taught them.

INTRODUCTION

The Four Rs for Successfully Parenting Adolescents

Most youth between thirteen and sixteen are unpredictable. Trying to figure out their behavior is like riding a roller coaster blindfolded. You're never sure exactly which way you're going: up, down, sideways, or in circles! One minute they act so mature, and a couple of hours later their actions remind you of the toddler years! Actually a teenager is similar to a toddler except now they have hormones and some even have wheels! The adolescent years have been described as a period when youngsters don't talk to the family, live in the clutter they call a room, and come out three times a day to eat and grunt at the family. Adolescence is a stage of life when children seem to want little contact with their family, but idolize their friends. No wonder parents compare trying to love a teenager to hugging a cactus! In fact, many parents look forward to parenting an adolescent about as much as they would to hugging one of those prickly plants! The following story reminds us why.

A Story

"I'll never forget the summer our son, Sam, turned thirteen," our friend Kristin told us. "We had just weathered several difficult months. Randy's new job as a marketing rep kept him on the road most of June and July, so I was left holding down the fort with our four children (one of them a budding adolescent) and their assorted activities: soccer games and practices, ballet lessons, and Little League—not to mention one big freelance writing job I had committed to finish before the fall!

"As a reward for making it through the hectic summer, Randy and I planned a getaway—to get away from our kids and to get reacquainted with each other. I made all the arrangements. Our three youngest children spent the week at the beach with some family friends, while my parents agreed to let Sam, our oldest, stay with them. As a new teenager Sam was excited that he didn't have to be with his three younger siblings, and he was also looking forward to earning some spending money by working on his grandparents' horse farm.

"Sam spent most of his time mending fences and working in the stables. At the end of each day, when my parents would invite Sam to go to dinner or to accompany them on some errand, he would answer, 'I'd rather stay home.' Mom and Dad understood.

"Yes, Sam was tired, but he had an ulterior motive," Kristin continued. "That summer my parents bought two new cars, a small tan Toyota and a dark green Acura. Unfortunately, they usually left the keys lying around or even in the ignition of the cars. Not smart!"

We could sense disaster coming as Kristin filled in the following details. Sam, like most young teenagers, was fascinated with new cars, especially the Acura. Even though he was still two years away from getting his learner's permit, he was relentless in trying to convince his parents to teach him how to drive.

That week in August, the temptation for Sam was too great. What a great opportunity to teach himself how to drive. So when his grandparents went out, leaving him alone—and the keys available—Sam began his driving lessons in the new dark green Acura. First he drove up and down their long asphalt driveway. Next, he drove to the field beside their house and circled around and around to practice turning. Finally, he got brave enough to drive on the hilly road in front of their horse farm.

One day during a hard rainstorm Sam hit a slick spot on the road and lost control of the car. Skidding off the pavement, he crashed into a nearby road bank. Bam! The front fender hit a rocky ledge. The car bounced off the rocks and spun around. Bang! The back fender bashed into the bank.

When his grandparents returned, Sam panicked and concocted the following story, "A terrible thing happened! Someone stole the car and drove it into the bank up the street."

Surveying the scene of the accident, his granddad just didn't buy Sam's story. Instead Granddad questioned Sam until he told the truth. Sam was scared and embarrassed, but his granddad lovingly reassured him. "Sam, we want you to know we love you, and we forgive you." Sam's grandfather knew that Randy and Kristin would be back in a few days, and he wanted them to handle any punishment.

Unaware of the "green Acura crisis" Randy and Kristin had a wonderful getaway. After picking up their three younger children who had a great week at the beach, they drove to Kristin's parents to spend the weekend and pick up Sam before getting back to the regular grind. Rested and relaxed, everything seemed to be going so well.

The first clue that all was not well appeared when Randy and Kristin drove into the driveway—they instantly noticed everyone was home, but the new green Acura was missing. Kristin's heart sank. Knowing Sam's fascination with cars she immediately asked, "Sam, where is your grandparents' Acura?"

"Ssshhh," he said, "I don't want the other kids to hear. Be quiet. I'll tell you later. Everything's okay. Believe me," he pleaded.

Sam's quick answer didn't satisfy his parents. When Kristin asked her parents about the car, they also avoided the issue. Randy and Kristin kept insisting on getting an explanation until Sam finally told them the whole story.

That night Randy and Kristin couldn't sleep. Kristin kept asking herself, *Where did we go wrong? Why didn't I tell Dad to keep his keys in his pockets? After all, boys are fascinated by cars.* Talking until the wee hours of the morning, Randy and Kristin began to realize that they couldn't lock up all the cars (and other temptations) in the world to safeguard Sam. He had reached an age that took him beyond their protection.

Randy and Kristin tried to look at the positives. Sam wasn't hurt, and neither was anyone else. No criminal charges would be pressed. His grandparents had been loving and forgiving. And in just a couple of days the whole family would be back in Virginia where no one would know what had happened.

But Randy and Kristin could not forget the negatives. Insurance would not cover the $2,600 it was going to cost to fix the car. Where would they get the money? Was this accident an indication of even worse things to come? How on earth would they make it all the way through the teen years of all four children when there was already a major crisis in the very first year?

The next day Randy and Kristin took Sam out for some frozen yogurt so they could talk without the other children overhearing the conversation. All were quiet as they began to eat. Finally Randy spoke. "When you were just a little guy, Sam, we could protect you. When you threw sand at a friend or threw rocks at cars, we could discipline you quickly, and there was never much harm done. But now the consequences are much, much greater. Another car could have been involved in the accident, and the people in that car could have been hurt. You could have been hurt or crippled for life or even killed." Randy paused. Sam's eyes fill with tears.

Kristin continued. "Sam, we love you. Still, we want you to realize the seriousness of this situation. And you can be sure other times we are not around, you will be tempted. What are your standards? Are you going to stand firm, based on your own convictions?"

As they discussed this crisis, Randy and Kristin felt that for the first time, Sam was beginning to feel that he had to be responsible for his actions. He had been scared enough by the accident that he seemed to want to avoid another big mistake if possible.

Randy and Kristin made it clear to Sam that they would pay the $2,600 to repair the car, but after he finished college, he was to repay them. Now they were faced with the question, Where do we go from here? Their first step was to be willing to forgive Sam—and then to focus on the future instead of the past.

Kristin told us, "We felt that Sam had learned a big lesson. If we didn't put this mistake behind us, it could become a noose around his neck. If we continued to think, 'We don't know if we can trust him,' he might begin to think of himself as a renegade. The rest of the weekend we didn't even mention the accident, the green Acura, or the $2,600. It wasn't easy, but we made it through the weekend."

"How did you manage to put it aside and not talk about it?" Claudia asked.

"See these calluses on my tongue?" Kristin laughed. "Seriously, it was hard. But we were able to move on to smoother ground with Sam."

Making the Years Golden

You may know how Randy and Kristin felt. Maybe you aren't facing a wrecked car, but you probably have your own version of their Acura story. Or, if your children are still preteens, you may not have faced a major problem yet, but you're already worried about the years ahead.

We all cringe when we hear statements like, "Better enjoy your children now. These are the golden years. They'll break your heart later." For the Arps, the elementary years had their high times; planned summers and projects contributed to sanity, but we wouldn't classify them as "golden," not with three active boys. As we approached the adolescent years, we already had *many* stories to tell; we wanted things to get better, not worse!

Don't misunderstand us; we had always wanted to be parents. Definitely overachievers, we had shelves of parenting and child psychology books to prove it. But the approach of adolescence caused us great apprehension, and we still remember feelings we had when our oldest son began to make teenage noises at eleven and twelve. Until then, we had thought we still had months before he was to reach the teens. The relative calmness (relative to the teenage years, that is) of the elementary years had disappeared, and all signs seemed to forecast turbulent times ahead. Would the teen years really be terrible? Or was there an outside chance they could be terrific?

Our questions led us to do our own research. We began to observe and talk with seemingly successful parents. What were their secrets? What were they doing right? We asked many questions, and we received much advice. As we sifted through the information, a few basics appeared, and the bottom line became clear: It's the relationship that counts.

Our friend Bill challenged us: "Keep the lines of communication open. As long as you can relate and talk to each other, both you and your teen will make it through all the other problems that come along. You'll be too strict in some areas and too lenient in others, but as long as you can talk about it you'll come out okay."

Another parent added a caution: "The relationship with your adolescent is the key factor. But it's extremely hard to develop that relationship during the teen years if you haven't worked on it previously. Build relationships with your children early. Do it now. Don't wait until later."

To make our relationship with our children the top priority for the years ahead, we felt we needed a reasonable plan for transferring privileges and responsibilities, so that we would be preparing our adolescent each year for that moment of full independence. Scary as it was, we realized with or without a plan of release, our sons would one day grow up and leave our nest. The challenge for us as parents was to help them leave prepared to face life as adults, while maintaining a positive relationship with us!

That year we set family goals placing at the top of the list our desire to strengthen our relationship with the boys—especially our new teenager. For instance, one of Dave's goals was to have a dad/teen breakfast once a month to discuss a specific chapter from the book *Dare to Be Different* by Fred Hartley. Each year after that we reevaluated the steps we had taken that year, discarded the ineffective ones, tried to strengthen the positive approaches, and looked for new ways to improve our relationship with our boys.

Friends began asking us, "How do you get along so well with your teenagers?" So we began sharing the ideas we had adopted.

Soon groups were asking us to speak at their meetings and retreats. After a while the parents in our sessions began asking for something more than just one- or two-day sessions. "We need encouragement from other parents on a regular basis—like each week," they told us.

These pleas led Claudia to form a MOM's Support Group so mothers could get together monthly to encourage one another and to apply positive parenting principles. The next year more groups started, so she wrote a discussion guide. The book, *Almost 13* (upon which this book is based), as well as our video-based church curriculum PEP (Parents Encouraging Parents) Groups for Parents and the secular curriculum MOM's & DAD's Support Group, grew out of our research and interactions with other parents.

While many of the stories you are about to read are our own, names and some details have been altered to protect the guilty and keep Arp adult family relationships positive. Also, we have included many stories and comments from parents who have participated in our parenting groups over the years. They were glad to have their ideas and stories included as long as their names also were changed.

As you read this book, imagine that you, we, and other parents are sitting in a room together discussing our adolescents. Some of the parents are almost through these years so their experiences tell us a lot about the times that lie ahead.

The suggestions and ideas of these parents and the opinions of experts in child development and child psychology, which are also included in this book, will help you prepare effectively for your children's teenage years. Now is the time to decide how you will guide your children through the adolescent years, not later when you are faced with a wrecked car or another emotional situation and are unable to think clearly.

You, like the Arps and the many parents who have participated in our parenting support groups over the years, need a plan for getting through the years ahead. Your plan may not be the same as ours. Our goal is not to give you a program, but to share with you some principles that worked for us and to tell you that these years may actually be the best years of all! We call these

es the "four Rs": regroup, release, relate, and relax. The
...s will help you develop a better relationship with your adolescents, one that will last throughout the teen years and into
adulthood. (In the following chapters we will be developing these
concepts in more detail.)

Regroup

By the time we had the answers to our kids' questions, the
questions changed. It seemed we were always regrouping. The
paradoxical statement, "We change in order to remain the same,"
certainly applies to parenthood and to parenting adolescents. We
constantly change the way we relate to our children over the years.
We didn't treat our eight-year-old the same as we did our toddler.
But it all happened so gradually that we didn't realize we were
changing in order to remain the same loving, caring parents.

As the teen years approach, once again you need to change
to remain the same. If you drag your feet or push too soon you
can mar your relationship. So as you approach the adolescent
years it's time to regroup again and to rewrite your job descrip-
tion. At this stage of family life, you need a plan. Start by ana-
lyzing your current situation by looking honestly at yourself, at
your adolescents, and at your relationships.

Release

Adolescence is, by definition, "the state or process of growing up." You need to prepare your teens to make their own decisions, which means gradually releasing decision-making power
into their hands. By their senior year in high school, teens need
to be making most of their own decisions—to practice this
process while they are still at home.

One dad commented, "The missing element with my kids
was this: Starting at age thirteen I didn't communicate that we
wanted to guide and develop them instead of control them."

Your challenge as a parent is to learn to release your adolescents so they can graduate into adulthood. We'll talk about two

great tools—the Teenage Challenge and Birthday Boxes—for beginning this process.

Relate

Once your plan of release is in place you need to look at some of the major obstacles that block communication between you and your children. What issues cause sparks to fly in your home? Curfews, hairstyles, homework, bedrooms, music, television, videos, clothes, makeup? You need to ask yourself, "What areas are really important? How my kids dress? The music they listen to? Their religious beliefs? The ability to withstand peer pressure? To stay away from drugs, drinking, premarital sex?"

We will tell you real-life stories and principles to help you answer the important question: "What will be the major and the minor issues at our house?"

Finally, you'll need to ask yourself another question: "Do the major issues coincide with what I am saying to my children every day, or am I spending so much time trying to perfect the surfaces of my children, that I am sending mixed and muddled messages about what's really important?"

Relax

It's hard to relax when you feel responsible for things you can't control. During the adolescent years we often prayed the serenity prayer: "Grant me the serenity to accept the things I cannot change, courage to change the things I can, and wisdom to know the difference."

One dad used to stare at that motto, which was written on the wall of the undercroft of his church. He knew it was true, but he didn't want to admit that there were things in his life he could not control. Finally, he realized that so many things in his life were out of control that he had to take the leap of faith. We'll be looking at just what we can influence in our adolescents' lives and how to relax and trust God for what we can't control.

Will I Benefit?

Perhaps you are asking yourself if a book can help you get your children through the teenage years. Obviously, we can't guarantee success. Everyone's experience is a little different and not everyone will see dramatic turnarounds. However, we are convinced that those parents who are able to build a good relationship with their adolescents will be better prepared to weather the storms of adolescence. We hope this book will encourage you, answer some of your questions, and provide many practical tips that will help you stay connected with your children during this turbulent stage of life. You may want to form your own parenting support group using the discussion guide at the end of this book or launch a PEP Group for Parents of Teens in your church or community. (Contact Marriage Alive [see p. 2] for information about the PEP Groups for Parents of Teens video based curriculum)

Listen to the experience of a mother who joined one of our parenting groups:

"Chuck was the kind of kid who could have gone either way," Lisa said. "The year he was in the seventh grade I was paralyzed with fear. He had never been a very good student, but he had been a star football player. Then he was injured, and he couldn't play for the rest of the season. His self-esteem was at an all-time low as he watched the games from the stands.

"Some of his friends were becoming fascinated with drugs. I could tell that for the first time his friends were influencing him. I was at my wits' end. Then I started coming to PEP Groups for Parents.

"First I found support for me. I felt like such a failure, yet here were other parents who were saying, 'My kid says he hates me, too!' I was also getting some help in understanding my son. I began to realize it was okay to overlook some of the negatives. His dress and slang vocabulary might not be what I would choose, but they weren't moral issues.

"I began to learn how to encourage Chuck and to let him know I was on his team. With football gone and no strokes for academics, I knew he needed something that he could do well.

That spring I made a deal with him. 'You go out for track this spring, and then you can play football next year.'

"Chuck discovered he was really good at the high jump. The more he practiced, the more he won. The more he won, the better he felt about himself. His grades began to pick up, and slowly he began to make a turnaround. By the end of the school year, we entered what we now refer to as the beginning of the 'up time.' Chuck was realizing he was an okay person in other people's eyes. I think my affirming him at home had a lot to do with how he perceived himself. His coach even commented, 'I've never seen such a dramatic change in a student in all of my years of coaching!'

"That summer we went to the lake, which got him away from the friends who were getting into drugs. I also encouraged him to swim competitively. By the end of the summer, he had become so good that he placed third in the city swim meet. My mom asked me why I was killing myself driving my kids everywhere. I told her, 'Mom, I'd rather drive than worry! If the kids are busy with track and swim meets, there's reason to say no when others want them to do questionable things.'

"By the time Chuck was in the tenth grade, his grades still fluctuated up and down, but he was a changed person. It's amazing what can happen when you get your eyes off yourself and focus on how you can encourage your kid. The principles I learned in my PEP Group for Parents and the support from other parents were real lifesavers for me. It saved us from some bad, bad times, and you can quote me on that!"

Challenge

If you are really serious about developing a relationship with your adolescents that will weather the teenage storms and last for a lifetime, begin here!

Think about your own adolescents. Is there something you already know you can do to improve your relationship? Who could you call this week to start a PEP Group with you? (Use the discussion guide in the back of this book to facilitate your group.)

PART ONE

Regroup:

Evaluating Yourself, Your Adolescent,
and Your Relationship

Will the Well-Rounded Teenager Please Stand Up?

What happened to my little angel now that she has turned twelve? What once was a smooth, friendly mother-daughter relationship has fumed into a volcano that is about to erupt at any time," one mother admitted in a parenting group.

"Fourteen was a fantastic year with Pete, but now that he's fifteen, instead of maturing, he's regressed. I don't understand!" a dad said.

Perhaps you can identify with these parents. The trouble with figuring out what your kids are like is that by the time you do, they've done another flip-flop. The only thing that you can count on during adolescence is change!

Changing Colors

One day Claudia asked our son who had just turned fourteen, "How do you feel about life?"

He shrugged his shoulders as if he really didn't know or care, but finally he said, "Well, I'm not satisfied with my teachers, my friends, or the world situation."

"What about you?" she prodded.

Laughing, he said, "I'm the only thing that's perfect!"

Claudia wasn't ready to let the subject be dismissed so flippantly. Really wanting to understand his feelings, she asked, "How do you feel about being a teenager?"

"I really like it. I get to be an adult without all the responsibilities like earning a living."

Persistence paid off. Sometimes your kids may open up to you with no prodding; other times engaging in a real conversation with them is like pulling teeth.

While learning to relate on a more adult level at one moment, our maturing teen a couple of hours later was playing "Capture the Flag" with his younger brothers. One challenge you face as a parent is to understand and accept teens who change like a chameleon, who put on different colors every day. It was easier to accept the changes that normally occurred between babyhood and childhood. Even the "terrible twos" were at least predictable. It is tricky at best to try to understand teenagers who are still in the process of trying to understand themselves.

Four Teen Profiles

Not only are teens changeable, they are unique. If your kids are like ours, you may wonder how children growing up in the same environment, having the same parents, can be so different from each other. One of our sons was so uptight and self-disciplined that he organized the lives of everyone around him. Another was so laid-back and relaxed that we wondered how he got out of bed in the morning. Yet they had basically the same environment.

A few years ago, after studying our adolescents and their friends, we came up with four teenage profiles (three of which were represented in our home). Being aware of these general types can help you to know what to expect from your teens and also to know that your teens are no worse than other adolescents.[1]

Sally Sparkle

Sally is popular at school, very outgoing, and fun. If a party takes place, Sally's sure to be there or at least to have been invited. She adds that special spice to family life, but sometimes things can get a little too spicy! She has a monopoly on the cordless phone, which has a permanent parking place in her room. What she would really like to have is a beeper and her own cell phone!

She comes with a set of friends who always seem to be around. What a bore for Sal if she is forced to spend an evening alone. She is uninhibited and impulsive—a scary combination for parents! She has good intentions, but poor follow-through. Like a butterfly she flits from one thing to another, leaving a string of unfinished projects and many messes when she finds something more exciting.

At school Sally tries to keep her studies from interfering with her social life, so the teachers describe her as "playful," needing to concentrate more on her work.

Take-charge Thomas

Tom, the organizer, is the leader in his group. You always know when Tom hits the door. He confronts and argues with his teachers—a gifted debater! Tom has enough self-confidence for the whole family. When questioned about his latest purchase and reminded that no one else is wearing such attire, he responds, "That's okay, I set the styles." Many times he is right.

Strong-willed and hardworking traits sometimes cause him to be domineering and to walk over other people—especially parents. He also tends to be selfish, relating to his world in light of "Tom" and his needs. He considers his brothers' and Dad's closets as his own and helps himself generously to whatever he needs. Patience and sympathy are definitely not his strongest attributes. His teachers enjoy his quick mind but could do without his sarcasm and "smart mouth," traits he developed at an early age. Without a doubt Tom is going to contribute to the world in one way or another.

Laid-back Larry

We all enjoy Larry's easygoing, calm disposition. His boiling point is so high he rarely gets angry, but watch out when he does, because he's not always sure of the appropriate way to handle it. His listening ear and dry wit make him well accepted at home and with his peers, but he is much quieter than Tom and Sally. Once on a family vacation Larry was left at a pit stop in Reno and not missed by the family for the next fifty miles!

Life for Larry is a pleasant, unexciting experience. His biggest problem is that he is s-l-o-w and unmotivated. He does not derive his sense of self-esteem from academic achievements. "Larry's so pleasant to have in class," his teachers say, "but can you do anything to help me motivate him to work harder and faster?" He tends to be the underachiever, but once his internal motivation clicks on, he has a steady consistency we all can admire!

Roller-coaster Renee

Renee is the ultra-responsible teen. She's quieter than her brothers and sisters, but she has a rich inner life. While Sally Sparkle's feelings are oozing out on everyone, Renee's feelings are directed inward. Like Sally, she is feelings-oriented and often rides her emotions like a roller coaster—high then low, up then down!

A deep thinker and creative teen, she sometimes amazes her parents with her insights, but woe to everyone around her when she begins to become negative and introspective. She convinces herself that she is unloved. Her teachers are quick to tell us that she is a good student, but they think she shouldn't take life so seriously.

What's Your Combination?

No doubt you can already see some of these characteristics in your adolescents, so now's the time to take a good look at your children's personalities. We found it helpful to consult a basic temperament chart (see illustration 1). Obviously such a general and mechanical analysis does not allow for the many individual combinations, but it does help parents to identify the basic characteristics of a particular child.

SPARKLER

STRENGTHS	WEAKNESSES
Friendly	Undisciplined
Responsible	Weak-willed
Warm	Self-indulgent
Talkative	Unreliable
Generous	Changeable
Spontaneous	Unpredictable
Impulsive	Restless
Charming	Unproductive
Sympathetic	Disorganized
Tender	Shallow
Impressionable	Fickle
Fun	Unfocused

TAKE-CHARGE

STRENGTHS	WEAKNESSES
Motivating	Domineering
Determined	Stubborn
Strong-willed	Rebellious
Confident	Hot-tempered
Bold	Reckless
Daring	Violent
Energetic	Sarcastic
Practical	Haughty
Quick-thinking	Crafty
Decisive	Vengeful
Persistent	Hard to please
Faithful	Unsympathetic

ROLLER COASTER

STRENGTHS	WEAKNESSES
Deep Thinker	Moody
Sensitive	Self-centered
Analytical	Sad
Creative	Negative
Idealistic	Pessimistic
Perfectionist	Haughty
Self-sacrificing	Easily offended
Genuine	Suspicious
Orderly	Vengeful
Faithful	Unforgiving
Self-disciplined	Impractical
Thorough	Seldom satisfied

LAID-BACK

STRENGTHS	WEAKNESSES
Calm	Slow
Cool	Lazy
Peace-loving	Easily stagnated
Dependable	Indifferent
Practical	Passive
Adaptable	Apathetic
Efficient	Detached
Good-natured	Dislikes inconvenience
Stabilizing	Self-righteous
Impartial	Proud
Diplomatic	Arrogant
Witty	Scornful

Illustration 1[2]

On this chart Sally Sparkle and Take-charge Thomas are the two outgoing teens, while Laid-back Larry and Roller-coaster Renee are more introverted. Where do your adolescents fit? Probably they are a combination of two or three, perhaps sixty-percent take-charge and forty-percent sparkle, or seventy-percent sparkle and thirty-percent laid-back. This is true in our family, but we have found that usually one temperament is dominant.

One of our sons was definitely a Take-charge Thomas. As a teenager he was determined and strong-willed, independent, courageous, and a leader—and a real challenge for his parents! Another son was a Laid-back Larry. Easygoing and likable, when things got tense at our house he would look around and ask, "Where's the humor?" (reminiscent of that great ad campaign, "Where's the beef?"). His one-liners helped to dispel a lot of tension. Although he was bright, school for him was a drag. "I'd never want to make all A's," he once said when Dave was discussing his grades with him. "It would be evidence of an unbalanced life!" Another son was more like melancholy Roller-coaster Renee. As a teenager he was an introspective, analytical perfectionist. He was the only Arp who ever walked around for days calculating his math grade and then was able to raise it from a D to a B in the last two weeks of a six-week grading period! While we all may need his quiet nudge toward excellence, we might add, however, that his perfectionism did not reach into all areas of his life.

Look again at illustration 1 on page 29 and assess your adolescents. Remember Larry will never be as motivated as Tom, and Tom will never be as sensitive to others as Renee. Studying your kids' personalities encourages you to concentrate on their strengths and, at the same time, help them overcome their weaknesses. It also helps you to manage your own expectations.

Next analyze yourself using the same chart on page 29. After all, you—and your spouse—are part of this equation. Take some time and reflect on how the temperament mix in your home contributes to parenting/relational outcomes.

Merton and Irene Strommen (he is a noted research psychologist, and she is a former public school teacher) encourage self-reflection in their groundbreaking book, *Five Cries of Parents:*

> Poor parenting can result from a parent's unresolved personal problems. There are brilliant psychiatrists and psychologists who know a great deal about the human personality but are inept as parents. Their insecurities and needs, obvious to others but not to themselves, profoundly influence their actions. Though insightful and effective when helping others, they lose their effectiveness when dealing with issues that touch their own lives. Having observed this phenomenon again and again, we find it crucial to encourage all parents to reflect on themselves as people and mates, as well as parents.[3]

Your temperament will affect how you relate to your adolescents. A "sparkle" mom may try to act too hip; a "take-charge" dad may take too much control. A "roller-coaster" parent may set too high a standard; a "laid-back" parent may be too permissive. Assess your own temperament and be as alert to your own weaknesses as you are to your children's.[4]

Three Parental Profiles

As we examined our own parenting and that of our friends, we noticed three different styles of parenting.[5] Now that you have some idea of your personality, see if you recognize your parenting profile. Actually we can compare parenting styles with the way we nurture plants. Consider the following three profiles.

The Smotherer

The smotherer wants to stay in control and help the adolescent avoid mistakes. Because of his fear, Sam shows a lack of trust and gives the impression that he is always trying to keep his son in the hothouse—closing the door as his son surges ahead toward independence. When plants are kept in the hothouse too long, they become weak and root bound. Even so with adolescents who are smothered; they may be unsure of themselves and unable to resist peer pressure. Also teens who are held back may resent and reject their parents and their parents' ideas.

The Pusher

An equally disastrous approach is to push your children out of your care before they are strong enough to survive on their own. Paula is a pusher; she expects her daughter to become an adult overnight and gives freedom too quickly, minimizing the need for the nurturing warmth of the hothouse. If tender young plants aren't given time to adjust, many will wither and die. Likewise, teens don't yet have the maturity to consistently make wise choices and often fall victim to peer pressure.

The Releaser

There is a balance between smothering and pushing. Rhonda allows for her son's need to flip-flop between maturity and immaturity, giving him independence in a safe environment. Young seedlings must be acclimatized gradually to the new environment in which they will grow by allowing them short times outside the hothouse where they can experience the real world—the sun and the wind and temperature variations. They must have a "hardening off" period, a period to adjust. Then, if they are properly trained for survival in the new environment in which they are to grow, they will thrive.

Children also need a "hardening off" period, which gives them limited freedom and increased responsibility for themselves and their behavior under the watchful direction of their parents. You need to release them gradually. Your interaction with each other, which is greatly influenced by your different personalities, will provide a foundation for helping your teens enter the outside world. (In chapters 4 and 5, we will be talking about a strategy for releasing your adolescents into adulthood.)

Applying This Knowledge

Now that you have taken a critical look at your personality and that of your adolescents, think again about how you interact with one another.

In our family, Dave is a blend of laid-back and sparkle. He is the easygoing, calm, relaxed guy. His sense of humor was a great asset with teens, but sometimes he needed a push to get him moving. Claudia is a combination of take-charge and sparkle. It was easy for her to try to control everyone and give orders. Hanging loose with teenagers was foreign to her nature, so she had to guard against being uptight and trying to regiment our teens. On the plus side, she usually got our family moving when everyone else was in neutral, and she was a natural encourager.

How does your personality type fit with the other types in your home? With each child, the relationship is different. For instance, our oldest son and Claudia were both naturally talkative, so it was easy for them to be close during his adolescent years. However, both were critical and sensitive, so it was easy for them to hurt each other. They had to learn how to seek forgiveness in their clashes. Claudia's relationship with our second son had much less conflict, since he was understanding and rarely critical. However, she had to avoid asking too many questions or he would quickly tune her out. Dave related well to this laid-back son because they shared similar strengths and weaknesses. But Dave had to work at accepting his weaknesses since they were similar to his own. It's disconcerting to see your own weaknesses being repeated in your child.

Each family dynamic is different. Unfortunately, you cannot pick personalities for yourself or for your adolescents. You can, however, observe and accept your own personality as well as your children's. When you understand each other better, each person's uniqueness becomes exciting.

Understanding Your Adolescents' Goals

Adolescents are made up of more than personality traits. As a parent, you must also be aware of their goals. If you understand the desires that motivate your children's behavior, you will be better able to understand their actions.

In an adolescent-parent study that involved 8,165 young adolescents (grades five through nine) and 10,467 parents, the Strommens identified seven goals that most adolescents intuitively seek to achieve during the teen years:

1. Achievement—the satisfaction of arriving at excellence in some endeavor
2. Friends—the broadening of one's social base by making friends and maintaining them
3. Feelings—the self-understanding gained through sharing one's feelings with another person
4. Identity—the sense of knowing "who I am," of being recognized as a significant person
5. Responsibility—the confidence of knowing "I can stand alone and make responsible decisions"
6. Maturity—the transformation from a child into an adult
7. Sexuality—the acceptance of responsibility for one's new role as a sexual being[6]

These goals are probably similar to your goals for your adolescents. However, friction develops when you and your children disagree about how to achieve these goals. (For instance, motivated by a strong desire to broaden friendships, your teens may be overly susceptible to peer pressure.) As a parent, you want to help your adolescents achieve these goals in acceptable and appropriate ways—by learning to understand themselves and the world around them, rather than by grabbing at instant and compromising methods to fulfill natural desires. The four Rs—regroup, release, relate, and relax—will help you to develop a logical plan to move your adolescents along this road to adulthood.

They Will Not Pass This Way Again

The adolescent years are times of transition. Teens seem to have one foot in childhood and one foot in adulthood. They're at that uncertain, in-between age that at times can drive parents up the wall. Parents aren't sure where they belong, and the teens don't know either. So don't allow yourself to get frazzled about the present stage they are in. By the time you get into a total frenzy, they will have moved on to another stage!

Remember the best news is

1. Each stage is necessary;
2. Each stage is temporary;
3. Each stage is leading to adulthood.

Don't panic when your relationships appears to be breaking apart. Every once in a while, your adolescents may throw an "I hate you" in your direction. Usually, you will be friends again within twenty-four hours. Don't gloat and feel cocky, either, when your relationships with your adolescents seem smooth. One parent wrote, "This is temporary!" and pasted it on the mirror in the master bathroom.

Remember what our son said: "I get to be an adult without all the responsibilities." Allow your teens to be free to think as adults and then to be free to play or react as children at other moments. Remember, teens are people in transition.

Challenge

Take a moment to assess the strengths and weaknesses for each family member as individuals and in relationship to one another; then consider what you can do to encourage strengths and challenge growth in areas of weakness. Think also about your typical interactions with each other. What are the potential positives and negatives? What adjustments do each of you need to make to enhance the positives and minimize the negatives?

Be sure to ask God for wisdom in this process. Here is a suggested prayer:

Heavenly Father, thank you for my kids and for the uniqueness you gave to them. Thank you for each of their strengths—help me to concentrate on that and to build my kids up in these areas. Thank you too for their liabilities—help me to challenge them to grow in their areas of weaknesses. Show me how to help my adolescents in these weak areas without majoring on them.

CHAPTER
2

No Strings Attached

Breakfast was a disaster. It was one of those Monday mornings when everyone was running late and Dave had already left for an early appointment. As one son gulped down his last mouthful of cereal before racing out to meet his ride, he said, "I need a pencil."

"There's one on the counter by the phone," Claudia responded.

"I need one too," his younger brother chimed in, "and I'm going to beat you to it."

Both boys pushed back their chairs and lunged for the pencil, the younger brother grabbed it and teased, "Ha, ha, I beat you!"

His brother snarled, "I don't give a fart!"

That did it! Claudia completely lost her cool. "I can't believe you would actually say something so vulgar. Guess you just don't give a 'fart' about anything, do you?"

A car honk announcing their ride to school provided a quick means of escape for our sons, but Claudia, totally frustrated, burst into tears. Sitting at the kitchen table that morning with the slammed door and harsh words still vibrating in her head, she realized she had just behaved like an out-of-control adolescent! Do your kids push your buttons? At those times, how can you accept them as they are—with no strings attached?

Remember when your children were little? Did you see things even then that were hard to accept? Children maybe appear too bossy or too lazy, too messy or too loud. Over the years perhaps you tried to work on overcoming these tendencies, but now your teens or preteens drive you and their younger siblings crazy and still are bossy, lazy, messy, and loud. Coupled with adolescent ups and downs, these traits seem even more glaring.

One mother said, "I have worked hard on accepting my husband unconditionally but somehow never transferred this unconditional love to my teenage daughter. One day it hit me: *You're not applying all you know in this situation. You accept your daughter on a performance basis. Your love is attached to strings: if she toes the line, doesn't embarrass you, and is a shining example to your friends, then you accept her.*"

Can you identify with this mom? It is hard enough to accept a spouse or friend who is an adult. How do you accept an adolescent—who is paralyzed by peer pressure, who is consumed with self, who is jubilant one day and in the pits the next—with no strings attached?

You can start by remembering how freely God accepts you.

A New Perspective

The most wonderful thing that you can learn is that God loves you unconditionally. He loves you, period, no strings attached. His love doesn't depend on your being a perfect parent and making all the right decisions. He loves you just as you are.

This total love can be the greatest motivational force in your life. You want to become all that God desires you to be—not from fear that God will reject you or be angry with you but from thankfulness that he accepts you as you are and sees you for what you can become.

Likewise, you need to accept your teens as they are—in transition, walking the tightrope between childhood and adulthood. Adolescents are in search of who they are and how they fit in; they are still under construction, developing physically, emotionally, intellectually, and spiritually. When you accept them as they are, then you can begin to encourage them to grow and become all God wants them to be.

Recognizing God's infinite love for you, you can dare to take the first step in truly loving and accepting your children.

Remove the Plank

The first step is to get rid of the negative. In Matthew 7:3–5, we read,

> Why do you look at the speck of sawdust in your bother's eye and pay no attention to the plank in your own eye? How can you say to your brother, "Let me take the speck out of your eye," when all the time there is a plank in your own eye? You hypocrite, first take the plank out of your own eye, and then you will see clearly to remove the speck from your brother's eye.

Parents can get so involved in seeing their kids' inconsistencies and faults that they cannot see their own. Take the time to deal with your own shortcomings and to apologize for your own misdeeds even when it feels more urgent to deal with the glaring faults of your kids. If you truly want your kids to reach their full potential, you must model for them genuine humility. This is no easy task. It takes great perseverance to constantly place yourself before God and others in honest penitence—but the reward is well worth it. Your efforts will bless you *and* your children.

Be Thankful for the Positive Qualities

Once you can see clearly, turn your focus on the good. Do your adolescents really try in school? Do they call you when they are going to be late? Are they trying to control their tempers? Are they trying to be more cooperative? Be thankful for the positive! In Philippians 4:8 we read,

> Whatever is true, whatever is noble, whatever is right, whatever is pure, whatever is lovely, whatever is admirable—if anything is excellent or praiseworthy—think about such things.

Too many parents dwell on the negatives, living as if the verse says, "Whatever is untrue, whatever is ignoble, whatever is not right, whatever is impure, whatever is unlovely, whatever is not admirable—if anything is not excellent or praiseworthy in your adolescent's life, think about such things."

One high school counselor commented that when kids hit the adolescent years their parents often become tremendous "flaw-pickers," pointing out all the shortcomings and faults of their teenagers. During those turbulent adolescent years this behavior can drive the young adolescent kids away from their parents and get them hooked into whatever is in vogue in the peer group.

Choose to dwell on your adolescents' positive qualities. By becoming more positive, you can encourage your teens. As you get to know your children better, you can learn how to adjust your behavior to complement theirs. Remember, it's the relationship that counts! Your teens will be much more open to your guidance and correction when they experience your love with no strings attached.

Besides, a teenager's world can often be a scary place with plenty of people to tear down and discourage them each day. Make your home a haven for your children as you seek to release them gradually into adulthood. Giving teens the freedom to make choices within safe boundaries will eliminate many stressful battles.

To rediscover what you love about your teens, do this second exercise: Make a list of all the positive qualities of your teens. You'll be surprised at how many there are. One word of caution: Make sure you do both exercises mentioned in this chapter. You must look at both the good and the bad to see your adolescents completely. After you make your list, keep it so you can refer to it on your "down days."

If you are open and honest and seek forgiveness from your teenagers, while also praising their strengths, you provide a model for them to follow.

A Model

Claudia tried to put these principles into practice. Sitting at the kitchen table that morning after the battle over the pencil, she knew she needed help to quiet her anger and restore her perspective. How could she get out of this mess? She realized she had to start with her own inappropriate reaction. So she followed the four-step process she had discussed in her PEP Group for Moms the week before. Here are the steps that helped her regain her composure and forgive both herself and our sons:

Step 1: Identify your inappropriate reaction.

It was easy for Claudia to recall our son's irritating behavior and her "less-than-positive" reaction. Her list looked something like this:

Teen's Inappropriate Behavior	Parent's Inappropriate Reaction
Argued and used inappropriate language	Became angry, yelled at him, put him down, and also used inappropriate language

Step 2: List possible appropriate responses.

Clearheaded now, Claudia could name alternative reactions she could have had to her son's misbehavior.

1. Remain calm.
2. State that his language was inappropriate.
3. Keep volume and tone of voice at normal level.
4. Deal with the use of inappropriate language at another time.

Step 3: Be thankful for positive qualities.

The next step was to concentrate on the positive. Because Claudia and this particular son were so opposite, she sometimes interpreted his easygoing attitude as indifference. Clashes like this one over the pencil often resulted. So to help her move from anger to acceptance, she listed his positive qualities.

1. He works on his grades.
2. He is finishing his Eagle Scout award.
3. He doesn't drink or take drugs.
4. He is responsible in his job.

5. He likes his home.
6. He gives me hugs.
7. He participates in our church activities.

Claudia looked over the list and thought, *Boy, I'm glad I have a son like him.* Her attitude and perspective were changing.

Step 4: Ask for forgiveness.

When our son came home from school that day, Claudia apologized. Then she explained why she had gotten so angry.

"Hey, Mom, I think you overreacted," he said. Claudia agreed with him.

By admitting your shortcomings to your kids you help them to understand you better—and they even respect you more because you can admit you are wrong. Realizing parents are not always perfect also helps kids accept their own shortcomings.

Later that afternoon in his room Claudia and our son talked and talked, and their relationship was restored.

It's not always easy to ask an irrational teenager to forgive you. When you find it is just too threatening to talk to your teens, consider writing a note like this one:

Dear Keith,

I hope you had a good day at school. Today, I have thought much about how negative I have been in the past several days. Without meaning to, I have concentrated on the things that aren't the way I want them to be. Everyone has strengths and everyone has weaknesses, and I want to focus on what is right in our family and in our relationship. Please forgive me for being so negative. I can't imagine family life without your great sense of humor or your wonderful smile. Do you think we can get back on a more positive track with each other? If you agree to give it a try, give me a hug or a wink.

Love, Mom

Does dealing with your inappropriate reactions work? Emphatically, yes. It is amazing how quickly communication can be restored when you deal with your mistakes.

Summary

As you accept your children for who they are, you create a climate where they can flourish. Keeping the perspective that much of what happens in the teen years is temporary enables you to deal with the inevitable skirmishes much more effectively.

Challenge

To help get your eyes off your adolescents' faults do the following exercise: Make a list of each inappropriate behavior of your kids—let your mind go wild; make a long list. (Perhaps your adolescent gives "messy" a whole new meaning.) Then beside each listing write down your inappropriate reaction—a much harder task. (Did you nag, sigh, yell, compare him to another teen whose middle name is "tidy"?) You may be surprised that your inappropriate responses are just as negative as your teens' faults.

After you have finished, confess your negative attitudes and actions to God.

Finally, decide what your responses should have been. Look over both lists and write down the reaction you hope to have in the future. Once you've thought through the negative ways you interact, you will be better able to stop yourself from having wrong responses in the future, instead plugging in more beneficial responses.

CHAPTER
3

Bird Legs, Braces, and Zits

Thirteen-year-old Jeff writes: "Please help me! I got one A, two Cs, and a D on my report card, which is great for a guy like me. My parents screamed their heads off about the D. I built a pretty good model plane, but all they saw is the mess in my room. I baby-sat my little brother the other day (for free). Instead of thanking me, they yelled because Larry broke the peanut butter jar. If I'd grabbed it instead of Larry, he would have fallen off the counter.

"They tell me I'm clumsy, lazy, sloppy, and they say, 'Can't you do anything right?' Then they lecture me on how I should change. I know I'm dumb and awkward. They don't have to rub it in. Sometimes I feel like I'm an eggshell: If I get one more knock, I'll crack."

Think back to when you were thirteen. Here are one mom's recollections:

"What horror fills my mind when I recall the beginning of my adolescent years! Skinny legs. Pimples. Perpetually imagining what others thought of me: Did they notice my crooked nose? My padded bra? The absence of a boyfriend to sit with at the Friday night football game? Why did I have to be a runt—small and skinny? And my eyebrows, why didn't God give me more? On top of all this—braces, too!"

The Adolescent Puzzle

You cannot totally ignore the holes and weak areas in your teens, but neither should you concentrate on them. An adolescent is like an incomplete jigsaw puzzle. In the last chapter we talked about what happens when parents concentrate on the negatives (the missing puzzle pieces), why and how to deal with personal inappropriate reactions to the negatives, and how to accept teens in the same way God accepts us—with no strings attached. Now, in this chapter we want to emphasize the importance of concentrating on the positive picture forming in your adolescent puzzles instead of concentrating on the missing or half-formed parts.

If your teen gets all As and Bs in school except for a C in French, what do you spend the most time talking about? Sure, he needs to work on French, but perhaps your student is just not great in languages. After all, as one thirteen-year-old son told his mom, "You can know over half of the material and still get an F." (Could it be that parents focus on the negatives because of their own insecurities? If your teens are weak in certain areas, are you afraid this reflects on you and your training of them?) Inferiority is the key word to describe these years; surveys show that up to eighty percent of young people do not like themselves. Many parents we have talked to say that the age span from twelve to fifteen is the most difficult time in life. "We have the gray hairs to prove it!" they say. Self-doubt and feelings of inferiority reach an all-time high.

Dr. Urie Bronfenbrenner, eminent authority on child development at Cornell University, was asked during a United States senate hearing to indicate the most critical years of a child's development. He knew that the senators expected him to emphasize the importance of the preschool experience, reflecting the popular notion that all significant learning takes place during the first six years of life. However, Bronfenbrenner said he had never been able to validate that assumption. Yes, the preschool years are vital, he said, but so is every other phase of childhood. In fact, he told the senate committee that the junior high years are probably the most critical to the development of a child's mental health. During this period of self-doubt, the personality is often assaulted and damaged beyond repair.[1]

Many parents with whom we have talked basically agree with Bronfenbrenner's statements, but they say girls often catch the inferiority disease before thirteen. We also know that some adolescents do exist who like everything about themselves. If you have one, rejoice!

Most agree that the two most admired qualities today are beauty and brains. For boys, you might add brawn. It's grossly unfair, but the intelligent, the attractive, the well-coordinated adolescent seems to have a built-in advantage. Still that child may not realize it. Once Claudia talked with a former Miss America who never felt attractive as she was growing up. Amazing as it seems, the beautiful, talented child also feels inferior.

Self-Image

How do you see your adolescents? Are they a big hunk of potential? Or do you just see the deficiencies? Believe it or not, your children's self-image will probably match your image of them. Sometimes parents have to believe in their children when the facts point another way. We have to "accentuate the positive, eliminate the negative, and don't mess with Mr. In-between," as the old song goes.

Consider Joyce's experience, a mom in one of our parenting seminars. "I was raised in a family where grades and academic achievement were very important. The two Cs I received in school were traumatic for me. I still remember the sinking feeling when my son, Harold, brought home his first report card. How could anyone make Cs in the first grade?

"I bit my lip and took several deep breaths; then I gave Harold a hug and said, 'Harold, this is a wonderful report card. You're passing everything! But there's also room for improvement. You have great potential.'

"At the time I didn't realize that this statement would be repeated year after year for the next nine years. Still I was convinced of Harold's potential, even when some of his teachers doubted it. Finally, during the last few years of high school, he realized that getting good grades was important to his getting into the college of his choice. The Cs were quickly replaced by Bs and a few A's. In college, Harold excelled academically. Why? He thought of himself as intelligent, just as I did.

"He had a poster in his room during most of his teen years: 'If you think you can or you think you can't, you're right!' I'm glad I chose to think that he could succeed academically!"

Even Inferiority Can Be Positive

Sometimes a healthy sense of inferiority can be positive. Most everyone feels inferior from time to time. A healthy sense of inferiority is knowing that there will always be someone smarter, better looking, more talented than we are. Too often parents can accept their own inferiority, but want their kids to be the best.

When we moved back to the States from Europe where we had lived for almost a decade working as consultants with a Christian organization, our boys were great skiers—living near the mountains, they had grown up on skis. The Knoxville Ski Racing Team recruited them right away. They began winning races and collecting trophies. Before long, they were competing in the southeast division. Here they met others who were just a little faster than they were. We had to help them realize that they weren't failures when they came in second or third or last, as long as they did their best and gave their all.

The Other Side of the Coin

Each person does some things well. Identify the areas in which your children excel and help them capitalize on those strengths. Be wary, however, of three pitfalls:

Pitfall One: We want our children to excel in our choices.

If Dad was a football star, he may push his son Pete in this direction when Pete would rather pursue gymnastics. Look for your child's natural bent. Since one of our sons always loved to argue and discuss ideas, we were not surprised when he was asked to join the debate team. "You're a natural!" we told him. "You've been debating with us for years."

Pitfall Two: We want our children to excel in everything.

The parable of "A Rabbit on the Swim Team" shows the fallacy of expecting your children to be good at everything.

> Once upon a time, the animals decided to start a school. They adopted an activity curriculum of running, climbing, swimming, and flying. To make it easier to administer the curriculum, all the animals took all the subjects.
>
> The duck was excellent in swimming: in fact, better than his instructor. But he made only passing grades in flying, and was very poor in running. Since he was slow in running, he had to drop swimming and stay after school to practice running. This caused his web feet to be badly worn, so that he was only average in swimming. But average was quite acceptable, so nobody worried about that—except the duck.
>
> The rabbit started at the top of his class in running, but developed a nervous twitch in his leg muscles because of so much make-up work in swimming.
>
> The squirrel was excellent in climbing, but he encountered constant frustration in flying class because his teacher made him start from the ground up instead of from the tree-top down. He developed "charlie horses" from overexertion, and so he only got a C in climbing and a D in running.[2]

Whether your adolescent is a rabbit, a squirrel, or another unique "animal," concentrate on developing his or her particular talent.

Pitfall Three: We push our children too soon.

When we moved back to the States, we were surprised to see organized dances for eleven-year-olds, soccer leagues for three- and four-year-olds, and tennis lessons for toddlers. Sometimes parents are so eager for their children to succeed, they push them too soon.

If children do everything by the time they are ten years old, what will be left for the critical adolescent years? Now is a good time to stop and evaluate your children's activities. Is your daughter grouchy from the pressure of constantly practicing to be a prima ballerina when she should be enjoying her friends?

You can encourage your children to develop their talents as long as you resist these pitfalls. Let your adolescents know you're on their team. Regardless of how your children feel about themselves today (their feelings may change by tomorrow), they desperately need your positive support.

Five to One for Encouragement

Do you realize it takes five positive statements to counteract one negative comment? For the next twenty-four hours keep track of the number of positive and negative statements you make to your teens. Too often the ratio of a parent's positive statements is one positive statement to five negatives, instead of five positives to one negative. And remember five positives to one negative is just staying even![3]

"Parents need to emphasize the positive—to affirm the things the kid does well, and for the most part, ignore the things he does poorly," says Jay Kesler, president of Taylor University. "It is far better to put the accent on the positive rather than to bandage up the negative. Ridicule always hurts, but a young person who is affirmed at home is in a good position to learn how to handle it."[4]

If we do not build up our kids, who will? Their friends? Probably not, since their favorite way of speaking is with cleverness and sarcasm, like the "cute quips" written in a teen's school yearbook: "To the useless hunk of junk," "To the weirdo," "To the girl with the incredible hulk nose," "To bird-legs Bonnie."

What about teachers? Yes, some teachers do encourage, build up, and affirm their students, but others are quick to criticize. Students hear comments like "Can't you do better than that?" "Are you stupid?" "Your writing looks like a five-year-old's." "I've given up on you." "Where are your brains today, in cold storage?" "How do your parents put up with you?"

Let's face it, parents are the ones who care, who can love a sometimes unlovable, often irrational adolescent. Parents have the potential to be one of the most positive reinforcing agents in their children's lives.

Be an Encourager

What comes to your mind when you think of praise? Perhaps you remember your great aunt Gertrude telling you, "Honey, you're so levelheaded. I'm sure you would never let something like that bother you!" when you were really quite upset about the incident in question. Instead of beaming, you sink a little lower in your chair. Not only did Aunt Gertrude avoid getting to know the real you, she insulted you. Too often when we think of praise, we automatically think of this kind of flattery and insincerity, which is not true praise. True praise is demonstrated by the following characteristics:

Praise is sincere, offering honest and positive evaluations of a person or activity. If you tell your daughter that she is the best soccer player in her school when she couldn't even make the team, she may doubt your sincerity. Furthermore she may not believe you when you offer a real compliment. Keep praise sincere, like, "Your room is so organized. It must feel good to have a place for everything and everything in its place. Good job!"

Praise is affirming what your teens are becoming. Goethe, the great German poet and philosopher, said, "If you treat a man as he is, he will stay as he is, but if you treat him as if he were what he ought to be and could be, he will become that bigger and better man."

How does this relate to adolescents? Remember to concentrate on the beautiful forming picture instead of the missing puzzle pieces. When your teenagers show real maturity or good judgment, slip in subtle compliments such as these:

- "I really look forward to your being able to drive. I believe you will be an excellent driver."
- "You are going to make a wonderful mother someday, you are so caring and sensitive to other's needs."
- "It's rewarding to be your mom (or dad), but I also like you as a person. You're fun to be with."

Do not forget to affirm your adolescents in front of others, too, but be sensitive not to embarrass your teenagers. You could say something like, "Julie is such a help when we have other families over for dinner. She is creative and sets a beautiful table! She has a real knack for color and balance."

Praise is verbal. We can have all kinds of nice thoughts about our teens, but the power of praise is not released until we verbalize it. How much praise power have you released today?

Make praise a habit by acting on what we learned in the previous chapter: Look for the positive and combat the tendency to dwell on the negative. It may help to memorize Philippians 4:8, asking God to help you dwell on the fine things in your teens' lives. It's never too late to begin praising your teens, but making praise a habit *will* take some time. Research affirms it takes approximately twenty-one days to develop a new habit and six weeks to feel good about it. A grumbler doesn't become an encourager overnight, but it is possible to change and modify our behavior up until the day we die! Challenge yourself to make praising your teens a priority.

Begin by Beginning

A group of parents in a PEP Group were studying how to better encourage their children. Sadly most admitted they rarely encouraged their teens, so they made a commitment to each other to give their adolescents five compliments in the next week. One dad at the end of the first week said, "It felt so strange to hear the words of encouragement and praise come out of my lips."

Try it. It may seem strange at first, but do it anyway. There are many ways praise can be relayed. Use some of our ideas or create your own.

Holiday Acrostic

One Easter we made acrostic plaques for each of our boys to express all the positive qualities we were thankful for in their lives. We used astro-bright paper, formatted each acrostic on our computer, and mounted each in an inexpensive frame from the local discount store. Our sons seemed to like them and even hung them on the walls of their rooms alongside their posters, sports awards, and other treasures. You could make an acrostic for any holiday or special occasion:

> # Benjamin is:
>
> *E* xcellent writer
> *A* dmirable
> *S* ki champion
> *T* alented
> *E* very parent's dream
> *R* eliable

Or use the acrostic idea for birthdays, using the child's first name for the acrostic.

> # HAPPY BIRTHDAY
>
> *D* ynamic
> *E* nergetic
> *B* asketball Star
> *B* eautiful
> *I* ndustrious
> *E* nthusiastic

The gift of praise conveys to your adolescents (and all of the friends that frequent their rooms): "My parents think I am full of positive qualities. Maybe I am!"

Let us add a word of caution. As your children get older, they may not be so excited about displaying your artwork on their wall. One day you may walk in and find some of your creations missing. Don't get upset. While they may now consider acrostics passé, the art will have served its purpose and will have reminded them that you think they are great. Your message of encouragement will continue long after the room decor has changed!

Notes of Praise

Frequent notes of encouragement are simple but meaningful. In our kitchen we kept index cards, a felt tip pen, and sticky notes in a drawer by the phone. With the investment of a minute or two, a note of praise can brighten anybody's day like the following:

> *Congratulations! Knew you could ace that test!*

> *Jack, know you feel bad about the geography test. It's a real bummer to study hard and not do well. I admire your good study habits and think you are super. Better luck next time!*

> *Know it was disappointing to lose the soccer game, but with your good attitude, you're a winner anyway!*

Again, be sensitive to the time when your kids begin to feel they are too old for notes and stickers! For several years each morning Claudia decorated one son's lunch napkin with a note and a sticker. He loved them and carefully peeled each sticker off and decorated his lunch box. By the end of the school year all you could see was a collage of stickers. Message? Mom loves me and thinks I am neat!

Letter of Praise

A birthday, a happy event, a sad event all can be good times to write a letter of praise. One friend wrote a birthday letter to her thirteen-year-old, expressing all the areas of growth she had seen since his twelfth birthday. Another mother wrote a letter to her son who was graduating from high school. She expressed her faith in him and emphasized two gifts she had tried to give to her son: the gift of roots and of wings.

One lucky teenager received the following letter on her sixteenth birthday:

Dear Julia,

On the occasion of your sixteenth birthday, I want to share with you sixteen things I admire about you.

1. *Pleasing personality*
2. *Sensitivity to others*
3. *Commitment to our family*
4. *Inquisitive mind*
5. *Creativity*
6. *Faith in God*
7. *Great sense of humor*
8. *Organizational ability*
9. *Leadership traits*
10. *Willingness to stand alone in the midst of peer pressure*
11. *Academic excellence*
12. *Athletic ability*
13. *Good sportsmanship*
14. *Honesty and truthfulness*
15. *Good writer*
16. *Being a good model for others to follow*

I want you to know I love and appreciate you. Happy Birthday!

Love,
Mom

Special Person Party

Parties are expected on birthdays and other important days but a "special person party" is given for no reason at all except to say, "I love you; you are great." It can be simple or elaborate, with gifts or without. The structure is not important, the message is! Here is one mom's story:

"The big track meet was in two weeks, and Carl had practiced for months. It was to be the highlight of his sophomore year. Three days before the meet he landed incorrectly while high jumping and broke his arm. Did his world fall in? You bet it did!

"The family rallied together. I made his favorite dinner. His sister baked and decorated a cake that said, 'Carl, you are our Super Star.' We made posters that said: 'We admire your spirit!' 'Next Year's Track Champ!' We each gave him a coupon stating something that we would do for him.

"Did this party erase the disappointment he felt? No. But it did express that we understood and felt his hurt and that we were on his team."

Easing the Hard Knocks

Our lives are sprinkled with disappointments, hurts, and frustrations. The adolescent years are times that are especially vulnerable to hurts and hard knocks. If we are willing to sprinkle our adolescents' lives generously with encouragement and to concentrate on their good points, we can be positive reinforcing agents who say, "You're very special. You are a person of value. I'm so glad I'm your parent!"

Challenge

Keep a record of the positive and negative statements you say to your adolescents for the next twenty-four hours.

Give your adolescents one honest compliment each day this week. List things for which you could compliment them.

Plan and write down one praise project you are going to do this week, such as write a letter, make an acrostic, have a special person's party.

PART TWO

Release:

Graduating Kids into Adulthood

CHAPTER
4

The Launching Pad

İt's tradition," Dave told himself as the rain pounded the tent. Visions of home and a comfortable, dry bed were interrupted by a twelve-year-old son who wanted Dad to listen to his favorite music on the boom box.

This was the third time Dave had braved the elements with a soon-to-be-thirteen-year-old son. The "camp out with Dad" was part of the rite of passage we refer to as the Teenage Challenge—a series of physical, intellectual, spiritual, and practical goals that usher an adolescent into the teenage years. Part of the challenge for each of our sons was to completely plan, prepare, and pull off the weekend camp out.

Change Parental Roles

As a parent, your job is to work yourself out of a job and into lifetime relationships. If the ultimate goal of parenting is to prepare children to function independently as adults, then you need to have a release plan.

"But adolescence is such a scary time to even think about letting go," Brandon said. "Plus, I already feel like I'm losing control!"

Another parent in our PEP Group responded, "You are losing control! That's what it's all about. But you want to lose control in a controlled manner!"

"As scary as it is," another parent added, "we're going to lose control whether we plan for it or not, so what can we do to get this process started on a positive note?"

"Kids come programmed for independence," we reminded the group. "Their job is to break away and become autonomous people. Your job, in part, is to let go. You need to communicate to your children that a day is coming when they will grow up and leave your home. Another significant part of your job is to help facilitate this process. So why not recruit your soon-to-be teenagers and work together?" we asked. "When your kids realize you are aware that they are maturing and growing up, they will be much more cooperative!"

Then we shared with the group a strategy for launching kids into the teenage years—a strategy that worked so well for us that we have shared it with thousands of parents in our parenting support groups and seminars. Suggested years ago by our friends, Paul and Phyllis Stanley, we used a one-time project called the Teenage Challenge to launch all three Arp boys into the teenage years. As a result of this experience, our children entered their teen years a little less shaky, a little more self-assured, and a little more positive. We might add that we entered this new phase of family life with real hope instead of a sense of impending doom.

The Teenage Challenge

Practically missing in our culture today are rites of passages—like the Jewish bar mitzvah. We have already discussed how parents (and the culture) push children too soon and how kids grow up too fast. When they hit the teenage years, they have already "been there, done that."

The onset of adolescence comes with insecurities and fears for both parents and adolescents. Both may feel somewhat incompetent. Most parents we talk to say they would invest the time and effort to prepare for the teenage years if they just knew how. And most preteens we talk to also would like their parents to acknowledge that they are growing up and not to treat them "like little kids." The Teenage Challenge helps to meet the needs of both. Here's how we used it at our house.

Several months before each son's thirteenth birthday, we presented him with a Teenage Challenge. We told him, "We're excited that in a few months you are going to be a teenager. We are entering a new phase of family life. No longer will we relate to you as a child—actually you are becoming a 'pre-adult,' and we want to build a more adult relationship. We also want to help you prepare for your teen years by giving you a Teenage Challenge."

Then we explained the challenge, which included goals in four different areas: physical, intellectual, spiritual, and practical. For motivation we told each son, "If you complete it by your thirteenth birthday, you will receive a reward."

We designed the challenges for each of our sons, presented the challenge, and then discussed it; but many other parents have effectively recruited their soon-to-be teen to help design their own Teenage Challenge, explaining the general concept and then saying something like, "I'd like you to think about how you would like to grow in each of these areas. Think of specific projects you could do. Then we'll sit down together, and write the challenge." Either way, you could take your preteens out for lunch to discuss the final document.

Along with this proposal goes an important message, "We are excited [instead of scared and anxious]! You are getting ready to enter a special time of life. You're on your way to adulthood. We want you to be ready for this new phase of your life, and this challenge will help you prepare. It is a big deal! You are going to be a teenager! We are happy about this!"

Positive excitement is contagious; infect your preteen with positive attitudes of anticipation, and also give the gift of advance preparation.

Be creative. Customize the challenge to fit your children's individual needs and personality. Perhaps one preteen has difficulty handling money, so you could challenge him to learn how to keep a budget, whereas another preteen has been a certified accountant since the age of six and has a fatter savings account than you do. Another preteen may need to polish up her swimming skills, whereas her sister was a starter on the swim team at thirteen.

Program the challenge for success by including challenges in areas in which your children are gifted and in areas in which your children have difficulties. You want it to be a real challenge, or it will have little meaning. Here is a sample Teenage Challenge:

Charlie's Teenage Challenge

I. Physical Goals

    A. Run a mile in under eight minutes.
    B. Learn to play a good game of tennis: work on serve, forehand, and backhand.

II. Intellectual Goals

    A. Read a biography about someone you admire, and give an oral report.
    B. Read one classic novel.

III. Spiritual Goals

    A. Decide what your own standards and convictions will be for your teenage years.
    B. Study the book of Proverbs and identify some helpful life principles.
    C. Memorize Psalm 1.

IV. Practical Goals

    A. Earn $50.00. Parents will match what you earn and save before your birthday.
    B. Plan and execute an overnight camp out with Dad.

Summer vacation is an ideal time to begin, since your preteen has ample time in which to complete the challenge. Our two older boys had September birthdays, so beginning the Teenage Challenge during summer vacation was perfect timing; our youngest son's March birthday worked well too. We gave him his Teenage Challenge the summer before his thirteenth birthday, allowing him plenty of time.

The timing can be flexible, but allowing enough time is essential. One parent gave her son his challenge two weeks before his birthday. Their house was in chaos for those fourteen days. Don't give a last-minute challenge; plan ahead.

When every item has been checked off the Teenage Challenge list, both parents and preteens breathe a sigh of relief. Now it's time to celebrate. Here are several suggestions:

1. Give the new teen a gift for a job well done. It may be a surprise, or the preteen may have suggested it. Some adolescents need more motivation than others, so it's smart to tie the challenge in with a gift they really want. Whatever the gift, the message is "Congratulations on a job well done. We are proud of you."

2. Provide a delicious meal using your new teenager's favorite menu. Include family and friends in the celebration. Make your teenager the star for that day.

3. Present to your teenager a "Certificate of Teenagehood," which can be hung in the teen's room (see illustration 2 on page 64).

The End Is the Beginning

The Teenage Challenge sets the stage for the coming teen years. Two benefits for the parents are

- a positive emotional start to the teen years;
- a greater sense of family teamwork.

The benefits for the preteen include

- a sense of accomplishment at the beginning of the teenage years;
- an increased awareness that parents realize he or she is growing up;
- a new and growing comradeship with parents and a realization that they are one team.

After completing his Teenage Challenge, one of our sons told us, "I like the fact that I really accomplished something." Another son commented, "In our class, only Joe [his Jewish friend] and

Certificate of Teenagehood

This is to certify that_____
has successfully completed all tests to prove he is
prepared to enter the wonderful and challenging
world of a teenager.

City_____

Officially Certified This Day

Of_____

"Trust in the LORD with all your heart,
And lean not on your own understanding;
In all your ways acknowledge him
And he will make your paths straight."

Proverbs 3:5–6

Teenage Challenge Completed

SPIRITUAL: Memorized Philippians 2:3–11

PHYSICAL: Ran a mile in 7 minutes, 46 seconds

MENTAL: Reported on the life of Mother Teresa

PRACTICAL: Planned and completed an overnight
camp out with Dad; earned $60.00

Parents' signatures

_____

_____

Teen's signature

_____

Illustration 2

I are really prepared to be teenagers!" At a time when so many kids feel insecure, you can give your adolescents the gift of confidence by preparing for the coming teenage years. So when you reach this challenging stage of family life, turn it to your advantage, and challenge your preteens. Both the adolescents and you will reap many benefits in the years to come.

Challenge

Develop a Teenage Challenge for each of your preteens.

1. Explain the Teenage Challenge to your preteens, and give them a copy of the sample. Ask your preteens to write down the goals they would like to set. If your preteens want your help, spend a couple of hours discussing the goals and projects together.

2. Go out for coffee or lunch with your spouse, or go to a quiet place by yourself. Look over the list of your preteens' strengths and weaknesses from chapter 1. List the positive areas you would like to reinforce. List the areas that you would like to strengthen.

3. Using these lists, formulate a Teenage Challenge for each of your kids, writing specific goals for these areas: physical, intellectual, spiritual, and practical.

4. Evaluate each Teenage Challenge by answering these questions:

- Is it practical? Have we added too much or too little?
- Is it programmed for success? Will it stretch our preteen, yet be obtainable?
- Is it measurable? Will our preteen know when the requirements have been met? Is there a reasonable time limit?
- Are the rewards clearly defined?

5. Make a date with each of your preteens for lunch or dinner. Compare the two lists and work together to combine them. Be sure to include items from your preteens' lists, and do not force your ideas on them.

CHAPTER
5

The Birthday Box

Becoming a teenager at our house was a big deal. After the family celebration, we planned another time to take our new teenager out to dinner with just the two of us. On this special occasion we tried to communicate the following message:

"We are excited about your growing up. You are now a teenager, and we want to relate to you on a more adult level. In five short years you will be eighteen and will probably be leaving for college. We want you to be prepared to make your own decisions, run your own life, and function as an adult. So, for the next five years on your birthday each year we will give you new and expanded privileges and responsibilities for the coming year. Our goal is that by the time you're eighteen you will achieve adult status—not only physically, but mentally, spiritually, and emotionally as well."

Then we introduced the concept of the Teenage Birthday Box and presented our new teenager with a small wooden box filled with cards—on each card was a new privilege or a new responsibility for the coming year. A typical thirteen-year-old birthday box might include the following:

1. CURFEW

YOU CAN STAY OUT UNTIL 10:00 P.M. with these conditions:

   A. IT IS NOT A SCHOOL NIGHT.

   B. WE KNOW AND APPROVE OF WHERE YOU ARE GOING
      AND WHO YOU ARE WITH.

   C. THE LIMIT IS ONE NIGHT PER WEEKEND.
    (FAMILY FUNCTIONS AND BABY-SITTING ARE
    EXCEPTIONS. CURFEW MAY BE EXTENDED FOR SCHOOL
    FUNCTIONS THAT GO LATER THAN 10:00 P.M. Check
    with us beforehand.)

2. PHONE PRIVILEGES

YOU CAN HAVE YOUR OWN EXTENSION PHONE IN YOUR
ROOM. (PLEASE BE CONSIDERATE OF OTHERS WHO NEED TO
USE THE PHONE!)

3. PARTIES

YOU CAN PLAN A BIG PARTY AND INVITE YOUR FRIENDS,
BUT PARENTS MUST BE HOME.

4. ROOM

YOU ARE RESPONSIBLE FOR THE CONDITION OF YOUR
ROOM. THE CONDITION OF YOUR ROOM IS YOUR CALL!
(THOUGH WE WILL NOT INSIST, WE'D LIKE TO SEE YOU
DEVELOP THE HABIT OF MAKING YOUR BED, VACUUMING,
AND DUSTING ON A REGULAR BASIS, AND KEEPING
CLOTHES OFF THE FLOOR.)

5. CLOTHES

YOUR CLOTHES ARE NOW YOUR RESPONSIBILITY. WE WILL
TEACH YOU HOW TO USE THE WASHER AND DRYER AND
HOW TO IRON. YOU WILL FIND A NEW CLOTHES HAMPER
FOR YOUR DIRTY CLOTHES IN YOUR ROOM.

6. MONEY

WORK OUT YOUR OWN BUDGET. WE WILL INCREASE YOUR
WEEKLY ALLOWANCE TO COVER SCHOOL SUPPLIES, LUNCH,
AND OTHER MISCELLANEOUS ITEMS.

While we didn't expect our new teen to achieve perfection with his box, we did expect him to take it seriously and do his best.

Then we gave our son a projected plan of progression which we hoped would motivate him.

We noted the progression from the center of the page (the thirteen-year-old birthday box he just received) to the outside of the page, which indicated independence, at age eighteen. For each year we had projected new privileges and responsibilities illustrated in expanding boxes.

At that point, we discussed the coming year's box, as well as the extended diagram. Nothing was in ink. All was negotiable. At this stage of life, we wanted our adolescent's input, and we wanted to work together. So, as our son gave suggestions, we were willing to adapt our plan to the point all could buy into it!

Warning! If the Birthday Box is only your input and your plan, don't expect your new teenagers to jump up and down and go along with it! This is a cooperative effort! However, we did communicate the following:

"How soon you move to the new level of privilege depends on how you manage your box. We don't think you're going to disappoint us. We're looking forward to watching you become a responsible adult."

How to Design a Teenage Birthday Box

Every Birthday Box will be unique, since some teenagers are more responsible than others. Here are some areas to consider as you design the plan for your teens' boxes:

Curfew

We began at age thirteen with a curfew of 10:00 P.M. one night per weekend. As the parents, we needed to know where the teen was going and who he was going with. Each year we added thirty minutes to the curfew, so at age seventeen the curfew was midnight and at age eighteen, the teen set his own curfew.

Many parents say their thirteen-year-olds really don't need a curfew as they are seldom out at night. Even so, it is helpful to establish the principle of the curfew before it is needed. Then each year you extend the curfew. Your sixteen-year-old, whose curfew may be 11:30, does not feel as restricted because the curfew is thirty minutes later than when he or she was fifteen.

Our curfew was not an ironclad rule. We made exceptions for special events and school functions. Also when a teen called home to let us know he was running late, we willingly added a few minutes. (We avoided most of those late night adventures, but not all!)

Academics, Homework

We began at age thirteen with limited supervision of homework and gradually worked toward their being totally responsible for their schoolwork. This was not the same age for each of our teens because some took schoolwork more seriously.

But by the time all of our sons were high school seniors, homework was their business (though sometimes they got their priorities mixed up). They learned a valuable lesson in managing their time, a lesson which benefited them as freshmen in college. Since they had already experienced being on their own academically, they were able to handle the freedom of college life.

Rooms

Once you put the care of your teens' bedrooms into their hands, it stays their responsibility. An occasional gift of a parent's helping hand will be appreciated, but sometimes it is better to close the door than to infringe on this agreement. This is a learning process.

In this area we have had very mixed results. One of our guys scored above average on housekeeping from the very beginning. Another lived in an unbelievable mess. Both got the picture: It's your responsibility, not ours. At least our boys knew how to do basic housekeeping jobs when they left home.

Grooming

Are personal grooming, dress, and hairstyles issues at your house? At what age do you feel comfortable letting your kids handle the responsibility for shopping and selecting their own

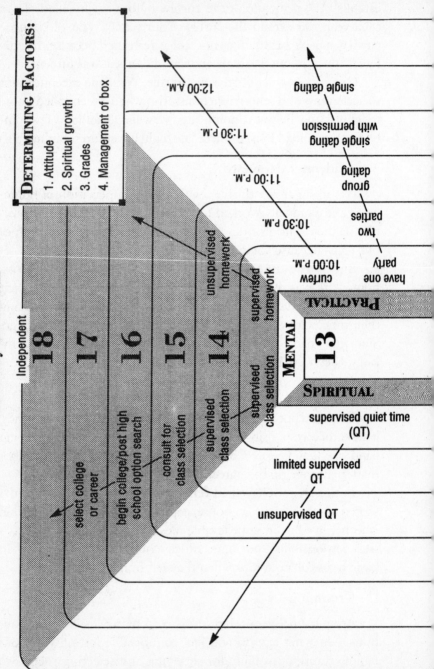

Birthday Box Plan

Independent

DETERMINING FACTORS:
1. Attitude
2. Spiritual growth
3. Grades
4. Management of box

18 — select college or career

17 — begin college/post high school option search

16 — consult for class selection

15 — supervised class selection

14 — supervised class selection / unsupervised homework

supervised class selection / supervised homework

MENTAL **13** **PRACTICAL** **SPIRITUAL**

12:00 A.M.
11:30 P.M.
11:00 P.M.
10:30 P.M.
10:00 P.M. curfew
have one party

two parties
group dating
single dating with permission
single dating

supervised quiet time (QT)
limited supervised QT
unsupervised QT

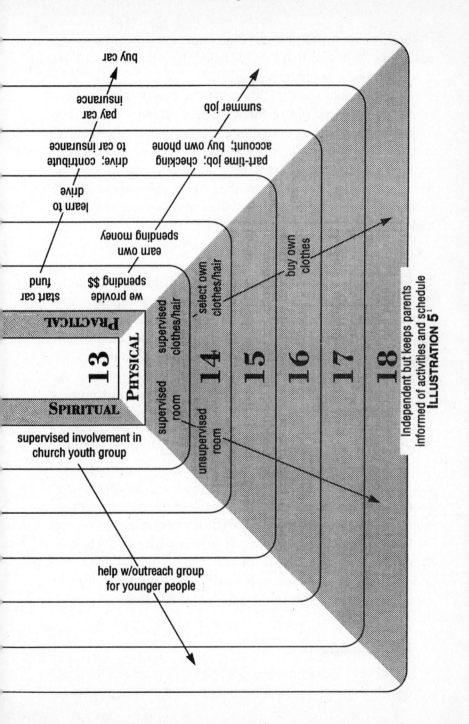

ILLUSTRATION 5[1]

clothes? From time to time our boys came home with the wrong sizes. One protested that "the salesclerk told me this knit shirt would get *bigger* when it was washed."

When are your teens able to wash their own clothes? We have seen sweaters come out of the washing machine so small they looked like doll clothes, even though we cautioned, "Look at the label before you wash it. If the sweater has to be dry-cleaned, we'll take it to the cleaners." We've also seen what happens to white underwear when it was washed with a maroon sweatshirt! Mistakes are part of the process. Too often grown men bring their dirty clothes home for Mom to wash!

Money

Some teens have a built-in knack for managing money; others have a knack for spending it. We started by letting our teens manage their money for school supplies and lunches. Once they showed signs of maturing, we added shopping for clothes and progressed from weekly allowances to monthly allowances.

We also included part-time and summer jobs in this area. At thirteen Joel mowed yards during the summer. At fourteen two of our sons worked as counselors at a Boy Scout camp. It can be difficult for a teen to get a steady job until he or she is sixteen.

Again, the standards we set varied for each son. With all his extracurricular activities, one of our sons simply could not work and still complete his schoolwork. Working, however, kept another busy and out of trouble. Obviously the teen's responsibilities at home will be less if he or she is working.

Once a teen begins to work regularly, consider letting him or her open a checking account. You may want to suggest that a certain percentage of the money they earned be saved for college or a special purchase. (You could include this standard as a part of the Birthday Box.)

Dating and Parties

To offset disappointment at not being able to date at thirteen, we put a tentative plan in their Birthday Boxes for when they could group date and single date. Seeing that these privileges were just around the corner kept them from complaining too much.

Spiritual Life

While you can't legislate what your teenagers will or will not believe, you can influence them! You can provide reading material—but forcing them to read it may prove counterproductive! In the early teen years we tried to help our boys find interesting devotional material on their level and included reading at least one of these books as one of their Birthday Box responsibilities. Check out your local Christian bookstore for devotional books and books on Christian beliefs and values or access the internet for quality web sites.

We also subscribed to *Campus Life,* a relevant cutting-edge Christian magazine for teens. The pages of this magazine were always dog-eared from use. You can check out *Campus Life* on the Internet at: http://www.christianity.net/campuslife. The *Campus Life* web site features articles from the current issue, complete past issues, message boards, and an offer for a free hard copy of the publication. You will find links to other sites (advice, humor, reviews, resources, trends, and stats), which makes this valuable for both teens and parents.

Another excellent web site is Screen It. You can log on at www.screenit.com and find reviews that evaluate songs, movies, and television shows by content, theme, and so on. It also provides a list of possible parent/teen discussion topics. This site can be a great help to adolescents who are in the process of internalizing their own values.

A third web site we recommend is www.search-institute.org— the home page for the Search Institute, which offers practical research, tools, and resources from an organization that's been studying teen values, attitudes, behaviors and needs since the 1950s.

Besides providing spiritual resources, we gave our boys opportunities to attend church-sponsored spiritual adventures such as youth conferences or youth group ski trips—another listing in their Birthday Boxes. The youth group at your church can be a positive influence. But what if your teenager hates the youth group? We know some families who changed churches to find a good youth group for their adolescents. One mom included the privilege of choosing a church in the box for her daughter's fifteenth birthday because the daughter was very unhappy at the family's church. That year the daughter became very active in a church that had an excellent youth group.

Again, developing a plan when the teen is young and still receptive to parental input assists in a gradual transition from parent's to a teen's own values and convictions.

Driving, Meal Preparation, and So On

Driving is a big privilege for a teen and often requires a full-fledged agreement within the Birthday Box structure. One parent in a PEP Group drew up the following contract together with her son:

Marvin's Driving Contract

Seat Belts
- I must wear a seat belt when I drive and so must all my passengers.

Passengers
- Only one other person may sit in the front seat with me.
- No more than three people may sit in the back.

Driving Range
- I may drive only within a twenty-mile radius, unless accompanied by an adult.

Restrictions
- If grades are below a C average, the car is taken away for all social events until grades improve.
- Any speeding or parking tickets I get, I pay for myself.

Miscellaneous
- I will always let my parent know where I'm going to be.
- No one else will drive the car.
- No one under the influence of alcohol may ride in the car.

[Author's note: We realize exceptions can happen when the only safe way for the teen to get home is to become the designated driver, but we would encourage parents to keep the general guideline.]

A driving contract sets the guidelines from the very beginning. We know one parent whose teenage daughter was very cooperative and mature; but when her boyfriend, who was a year younger, pleaded to drive, she let him. He drove too fast in a twenty-mile-per-hour zone, and the two teens were stopped by the police, who informed them that a teen with a permit cannot drive a car unless the licensed driver has been driving over a year. It had never occurred to the mother that her daughter would allow anyone else to drive the family car. With a prearranged driving contract, there would have been no question about the family's rules of the road.

You may also want to include other areas in your teen's Birthday Box, such as meal preparation, sewing, and simple car mechanics. When one of our boys was a junior in high school, he met a goal by reading a book about investments and making an imaginary investment in the stock market. Whatever areas you choose to include, the goal is the same: to develop the teen's competence to function productively in the adult world.

Finding Unique Boxes

During the year we keep our eyes open for unique boxes. We've found several interesting boxes made of various materials.

Our boys displayed their boxes in their rooms and use them to store their personal items. By the time they reached seventeen, they had five unique boxes, each a reminder of their growth toward independence. (Not all teens will keep their boxes on display!)

Monitoring the Box

Plan a quarterly or biannual evaluation with your teens to discuss how they are doing. If they lack self-discipline, you may want to get together more often.

Be sure to acknowledge successes along the way. One of our boys regularly asked, "How am I doing?" Since he had been doing very well, we hadn't thought to mention the box. After a few of his comments, though, we realized he needed some positive feedback, so we made a point to offer specific words of praise.

What if your teens abuse the privileges or don't carry through with the responsibilities? If all else fails, give them the same box next year. If they fail in one area, just repeat that area. Remember your teens want new privileges. Once they understand that privileges are accompanied by responsibilities, we expect they will not let you down.

One of our sons was the classic academic underachiever. Since he was bright we made his achieving a B average a requirement for getting his driver's license. "Gee, Mom, I grew up in Austria. You can't drive there until you're eighteen, so it's no big deal," he replied. When his friends began to get their licenses, however, his attitude changed. Suddenly his grades began to improve.

With this son, we found we needed to be flexible. Once we saw improvement in his grades and his attitude toward his studies, we allowed him to get his license—even though he did not have a B average—but limited his driving to work and to youth group activities. A year later he finally achieved a B average, and we received the good student discount on our insurance.

A caution: Before you tie grades into privileges, ask yourself, "What is reasonable for my teen?" Some kids work harder to maintain a steady C average than others do to make straight A's.

Some privileges can be sped up by a teen's excelling in an area. For instance, one son, who at an early age was a good manager of finances, had a checking account at fifteen instead of sixteen.

Alternative Approaches

You may want to begin the Birthday Box at eleven or twelve, or perhaps your teen will enjoy the box at thirteen, but not again at fourteen, or will not cooperate if the Birthday Box is begun at fifteen. Some of the parents in our PEP groups and seminars adapted it as a High School Box with freshmen, sophomore, junior, and senior privileges and responsibilities.

One mom learned about the Teenage Challenge and Birthday Box right before her son's fourteenth birthday, so she combined the two. The important thing is to set up a well-defined, progressive structure for increasing responsibilities and privileges each year.

One Family's Story

Mary smiled as she handed a paper to her son Brian. He had been waiting eagerly for it and nearly snatched it from her hand. He started reading immediately.

Brian hung the document on his bedroom wall and worked hard to achieve these responsibilities. Mary shared similar expectations with her older son, Curtis. On his sixteenth birthday, she took him out to dinner to discuss what he still needed to learn before he left home in approximately twenty-four months. Together they made a list, and now Curtis is taking care of his clothes and among other things, learning how to cook pasta and other basic foods. But the story doesn't end there. Mary's nine-year-old daughter caught the vision and decided to get a head start. That summer Megan listed her own goals, one of which was to place in an event in the city swim meet. She not only

---

Brian's Steps to Adulthood (age 14)

1. You may choose your clothes and hairstyle.
2. Your homework will no longer be supervised, but we will be glad to help if asked.
3. Your bedtime is extended until 10:30 P.M. on school nights.
4. You will receive $60.00 allowance a month for spending money and school obligations. Extra money may be earned by doing yard- or housework.
5. Your room is now your responsibility. Mom has the right to refuse to allow friends to visit if your room isn't clean.
6. You are responsible for the care of your clothes. Mom will teach you how to use the washer and dryer.

I know you can do it. I love you.

Mom

placed in several events, but also received the "Most Improved Swimmer Award" for her local swim team. "Megan was the only swimmer in our club that made and met her personal goals!" her coach told Mary at the awards dinner.

The whole family benefitted and grew as Mary encouraged healthy independence in her kids.

Why Not Take a Chance?

Wise parents begin working toward their offspring's independence almost from the moment the child is born. Just as you hand the baby a spoon for eating, knowing he or she will probably plaster the wall with food, so you take risks throughout their lives. Much frustration for both the teen and parent can be eliminated by releasing areas of responsibility and freedom once the child becomes thirteen.

Challenge

Establishing Teenage Birthday Boxes

1. Make a list for each teen of all the things they need to know before they leave home.

2. By each area indicate when you think your teens will be ready to assume the responsibility.

3. Sketch a box diagram for each teen, using the illustration on page 71 as a guide. Insert the different areas and potential progression. (Make a copy of each for yourself before you give them to your teens.)

4. Answer the following questions:

- Am I releasing too much or not enough freedom to my teen?
- Am I giving my teen too much or not enough responsibility?

PART THREE

Eliminating Major Obstacles

CHAPTER
6

Getting Off the Lecture Circuit

I'm a good student, chairman of the debate team, and a starter on the basketball team," said sixteen-year-old Jason. "You'd think my dad would be proud of me. When I was nominated for student body president, I was really excited. I came right home and told my dad and he said, 'Great, now change your clothes, so you can wash the car. You were supposed to wash it yesterday.' He's always too busy to listen."

Fourteen-year-old Nancy's experience was just as frustrating. "I open up and talk to my mom. She thinks she listens, but she really just waits for an opening so she can give me morality lecture no. 395. I just have to stand there and wait for the benediction!"

If these conversations represent typical parent-teen communication, it's time for parents to get off the lecture circuit. From parenting three adolescents, we learned you can't have positive parent-teen relationships if you don't listen to your kids. Our advice would be: Listen, don't lecture!

Think about your best friend. Are you too busy to listen to that person? Do you give sermons when you agree? Do you correct grammar when your friend tells you a story? Parents long for their adolescents to communicate with them, but too often when their kids begin to open up, parents are too preoccupied with thoughts of their own. One parent put it this way: "I see their mouths moving, I nod and say the appropriate 'Really,' 'Uh huh,' but too often my mind is miles away—or I'm distracted with worry about the next problem up the road."

One young boy who was competing with his siblings for Mom's attention held her face in his hands so she had to look at him and listen to what he said. Most adolescents won't go to this extreme, but they need your full attention when they talk to you.

Sometimes just the opposite is true. Sandy confided, "I listen to my thirteen-year-old daughter too intently. I analyze everything she says. Then when I see any rebellious or abnormal tendencies, I panic! And since my daughter loves the shock effect, I often end up being her guinea pig."

So how can parents get off the lecture circuit and really listen to their adolescents? We have three suggestions: resist giving a lecture, give your adolescent some space, and look for ways to draw out your teen.

Resist Giving a Lecture

A mom in a PEP Group shared this story: "I had pulled my shoulder in a tennis match and was in great pain as my thirteen-year-old son, Dan, began to tell me about a conversation with a teacher he not only liked but admired. 'Mr. Brown said only uneducated people believe the Bible is reliable. He even showed me some contradictions I'd never seen before.'

"Now a sick feeling in the pit of my stomach, which came from feelings of parental failure, joined the pain radiating from my shoulder. At the ripe age of thirteen, was Dan ready to shuck all my husband and I had taught him about the Scriptures because a favorite teacher believed differently?

"Somehow I managed to listen without openly showing panic. I remember saying something like, 'That's interesting. Where did your teacher get his information? We have several books that deal with this subject—perhaps you would like to study them. It's important for each of us to know what we believe and why. I wouldn't want you to base your belief in Scripture on what I say or doubt the Bible based on what a teacher has to say. You need to examine the facts for yourself!'

"Then silently I sent a giant SOS and asked God to help me trust him and not attack Dan or his teacher. How hard it is for me to trust when it seems all I have tried to instill in my teen is suddenly going down the drain!

"Later I gave Dan some books. His response to my suggestion that he browse through them was, 'Oh, Mom, I really do believe the Bible is reliable. I just wanted to see how you would react to someone who believed differently.' Whee, this time I passed the test!"

Dan's mom did follow up this episode by using Josh McDowell's excellent book *Answers to Tough Questions* as discussion starters. For the next couple of weeks they discussed one question each morning at breakfast. And during those discussions, she had to remember to resist reacting to every comment Dan made.

In a recent parenting conference, one parent said, "When my teenage daughter asks a question, I have a thirty-second opportunity to share my wisdom. Think about it," she reasoned. "How long does a television commercial take to sell us the latest detergent or soft drink? That's about how long our kids will listen to us!"

"And you never know when your teenager is going to ask a philosophical question," a dad added. "Just last week, I was driving my daughter to the mall when out of the blue she asked, 'Dad, what's the meaning of life?' I was flabbergasted! How do you respond to that one in thirty seconds?"

"How did you answer her?" the other parents wanted to know.

"Basically I told her, 'That's a question people have been asking since the beginning of time and each person has to come up with his or her own answer. For me, the meaning of life is linked to faith in God who created life. What do you think?'"

Think ahead through major issues, and prepare thirty-second mental outlines of your thoughts for those rare occasions when your adolescents ask for your wisdom.

Listen, Don't React

Sometimes when we do listen, we overreact to what we hear. In James 1:19, we are told to "be quick to listen, slow to speak and slow to become angry." During the adolescent years at our house we shortened and paraphrased this verse to three words: "Listen; don't react!" Then we posted it on our refrigerator.

It's a privilege to have a young person ask your opinion. A few poor responses may discourage any future sharing, so be careful. Sometimes the best response is to answer a question with another question like, "What do you think might work?" or "What are the options?" Questions like these will encourage your adolescents to think on their own and to come to their own good conclusions.

Consider one smart technique shared by a teenage daughter. "My mom has this wonderful way of getting through. She doesn't say, 'You should' when I need help with a decision, but 'Have you considered . . . ?' or 'Maybe this would work . . . ,' giving me the final choice. And she lets me rattle on with just enough encouragement, until I sort things out."

No Advice, Please

Sometimes when your adolescents talk to you, they don't want your opinion; they only want you to listen. Fifteen-year-old Kevin told us, "My dad listens to me, but he takes what I say and uses it as a launching pad for a lecture. I told him about a friend who was experimenting with drugs. I wanted to know how to help him. What did Dad do? He launched into a big lecture on 'teenagers on drugs, how awful' as if I was the one experimenting! Why does a friendly talk always have to turn into an object lesson? I just wanted to help my friend."

When your adolescents talk to you, they want you to hear them out completely with no interruptions. Once you begin to listen with an open mind and closed mouth, you can begin to listen for feelings.

One couple's story illustrates this well:

"I'll never forget my distress when our son Mark told his younger brother Jon, 'Go to bed. I want to talk to Mom and Dad.' At that point I braced myself for whatever was coming, something that couldn't be shared with a younger brother.

"'You know, spring break's coming soon,' Mark began. 'Some of the guys asked me to go to Florida with them.'

"Mark was sixteen at the time, and my husband and I weren't prepared for this pitch for independence.

"'Maybe all of us could go together,' I suggested after a long pause. 'You know, the whole family. Maybe Marie might even be home from college.'

"Mark shifted his weight from one foot to the other, cleared his throat, and said, 'Mom, it's not our house I want to get away from. It's the contents.'

"That statement threw me for a moment. I started to say, 'Well, that's a great thing to say!' Then I caught myself. What feelings was I really hearing? First, it was obvious Mark wanted a break from his family. Did he really dislike us, or was it just a cry for independence?

"'Give us a chance to think about it,' I said.

"That night as my husband and I discussed the idea, we thought of a possible solution. Evan, the Young Life youth worker who led Mark's small group study, just might go with the boys.

"'They'd accept him,' my husband said. 'They all enjoy being with him, and we can trust his supervision.'

"Did this negotiation take a lot of time? You bet it did. Along the way, Mark looked upward and jokingly said, 'They're great parents, God, but sometimes I wish I had the kind who don't care.'

"In the end, Mark, Evan, and four other teenage boys spent five days at the beach in Florida. They had a great time and, although Mark has never admitted it, Evan was a major contributor to their fun. They spent long hours on the beach; they rented a VCR and overdosed on fifteen movies."

Mark's parents found a solution they all could be happy with by being willing to listen to their son's feelings. How can you listen for feelings without overreacting?

Listen for Feelings

Listening for feelings means that you don't evaluate, don't offer advice, don't analyze, and don't ask tons of questions—admittedly hard to pull off. Listen with your mouth clamped shut, then feed back comments that let your teens know you are trying to understand what they mean and how they feel. Check out this typical parental response contrasted with a more appropriate response:

Teen: "Melanie is a complete nerd, she's two-faced and a fake."

Parent (normal response): "How do you know Melanie is a fake and two-faced? How would you like to be called a nerd? It's wrong to judge others!"

Parent (response when listening for feelings): "Sounds like you and Melanie are on the outs. It really hurts when friends seem to turn against you."

Stop for a moment and think how wonderful it is when someone really understands and cares how you feel. Everyone can handle pressure better if they know even one other person understands. You can be that "other person" for your adolescents if you are willing to listen—not lecture, react, or advise—and identify with their feelings. Save your advice for the family dog!

Give Some Space

Not only do we meet many parents of adolescents who are "natural lecturers," but also many who are just too nosy and intrusive. Restrain your craving for knowledge about your teenagers. If you have developed good communication, you don't have to read your daughter's diary, letters, and notes or look in your son's private drawer or locked box to check on behavior. You will surely lose your teens' trust. You might get information, but it's not worth the cost.

One mom shared this suggestion in a PEP Group: "My pre-teen daughter has one drawer that is hers; it is off-limits to me and everyone else in our family. As much as I would like to know what she has in her drawer, I have vowed not to invade her privacy. Since she has her private space, she's more willing to talk to me about other things."

Resist Snooping

"I was addicted to snooping," one parent admitted. "I investigated every dirty jeans pocket, every crushed piece of paper. I have even been known to spend up to an hour scotch-taping a mutilated note back together. Was I wrong? Oh, yes! Am I now reformed? I hope so!"

Perhaps your adolescent's room, desk, diary, and dirty jeans pockets should be labeled: "Snooping not allowed! Snoopers will be prosecuted!" Your children need privacy; they need to be given space. One reformed snooper shared the following:

"When our children began to enter the adolescent world, my wife and I began to pray that God would show us the important mistakes they were making. It's amazing how our prayers have been answered: a cigarette left on the couch; a comment from another mom: 'Oh, yes, your son is known as the "dirty word dictionary."' God has been so faithful in this area that we don't want to know what we don't need to know. Now as our teens are approaching the adult years, from time to time they share with us some of the things they did when they were thirteen and fourteen, and we are also thankful we did not know everything!"

A word to the wise: The early adolescent years (ages twelve to fourteen) often bring with them a fascination for dirty words and inappropriate sexual terms. If you accidentally find a filthy note, don't panic! You have not failed at parenthood. Do not take this note as evidence that your kid is into sex or drugs. If you found it legitimately, you can use it to open a discussion as to appropriate language, scriptural principles of sexuality, and controlling thoughts. But remember to listen, don't react!

When one of our sons was thirteen, we heard through the grapevine that he was using inappropriate language at school. Claudia mentioned her concern in a letter to a trusted friend who had older teens. Our friend's response was very helpful. She wrote:

"My feeling is there's a ninety-nine percent chance it's very temporary, and he's doing it a few times to get attention. We don't expect our kids never to make a mistake. But there's always a sick, scary feeling when we learn that one of our kids has misbehaved; we are afraid every mistake will turn into a lifetime habit. . . . Instead of confronting him personally, why not discuss the use of inappropriate language in a family discussion?"

We tried this, but Dave eventually had to confront him directly. He replied, "Dad, what if I promise not to use any more bad language as your birthday present?"

Dave heartily agreed. This promise was one of the best presents Dave ever received. (We're not saying our son had a hundred percent success rate, but at least he was making an effort to clean up his act!)

Give Physical Space

During the preadolescent years, our sons shared a large room partitioned into three cubicles. When our oldest son turned thirteen, we saw his need for space and privacy from two younger brothers. Our solution was to give him a new room on his fourteenth birthday, moving Dave's office to the den to provide the needed space. The inconvenience for Dave, although significant, was worth the benefit to our son (and his brothers).

It's not always possible to find or build private bedrooms for your teens. However, do whatever you can to create *some* private space for them. Adolescents need a place to call their own, even if that means building walls and making one bedroom into two or using room dividers or bookcases. Physical space contributes to good communication.

Give Emotional Space

Teenagers are noted for their mood changes. At times they are argumentative and irritable. They are more behavior-oriented than verbal, since they haven't yet mastered good communication skills—it takes a lot of energy to control their impulses as they strive for independence. Therefore, they need emotional space.

Are you willing to resist the urge to correct every angry word or action? Are you willing to let your adolescents vent emotions? Home is one place where kids should be able to blow it and still be loved and accepted. As one of our sons put it, "Home is where you prepare for the battle, not where you fight the battle."

One mother told the parents in her PEP for Parents of Teens Group, "This week Sean came in the door, threw his books on the kitchen table, and exploded: 'My dumb math teacher gave us a surprise test today, and I know I flunked! I hate him. I hate school. I am going to just give up!'

"After our discussion last week about how every slammed door and every angry word doesn't need to be corrected, I was able to respond, 'Sounds like your day was a real bummer.' Looking totally surprised, Sean said, 'Yes, it was!'"

Allow the luxury of venting some emotions. Why not practice the principle of love found in 1 Corinthians 13:4–5: "Love is patient, love is kind. . . . it is not easily angered, it keeps no record of wrongs."

As we focus on our teens more as emerging adults and less as children, we can begin to let them assume some responsibility for their actions, so we are not obligated to correct every fault we see.

We are not saying adolescents should habitually be allowed to slam doors or hurl angry words at their parents and other innocent bystanders. Neither should parents tolerate disrespect. However, often parents ride too hard on their kids because they're afraid they'll lose control of the kids. As a result, the teens are not given the opportunity to express their real feelings.

"I've learned," another PEP parent shared with the group, "that I don't always have to have the last word. My son may go off mumbling about how unfair I am. His mumbling doesn't change my position or the outcome of the conversation, but it does allow him a way to vent his strong emotions."

Once when one of our sons was visiting a home of a family with several teenagers, he commented, "You wouldn't believe it! Jim's parents never listen to how he feels about anything. They just state their case and say, 'That's the way it is. No discussion.' I sure would hate to live in their home."

We found that allowing our teens emotional space was the first step in making the transition from the vertical parent/child relationship to the horizontal friend/friend relationship, which now exists between us and our adult children. Adult friendships are based on individuals relating to each other as peers—not as superiors and subordinates. The process of getting to this kind of relationship with your kids is not easy, but if you work at communicating with your adolescent and at maintaining the relationship during the adolescent years, trust us, it is possible!

A friend of ours sadly related how her own relationship with her mother never changed from the parent/child relationship to a friend/friend relationship, although she is now forty and has two children of her own.

"To Mom, I'm still her little girl," she told us. "She gets upset if I try to build an open relationship by sharing opinions and feelings with her that are different from her own. To disagree, in her eyes, is to be disrespectful—after all, she is my mother. How I wish she could also be my friend!"

It's too bad this mother didn't learn to allow her daughter to voice some of her opinions in her teen years. How different their relationship might be today.

Drawing Out Your Adolescent

What about the adolescents who clam up and just won't talk? How can you foster communication? Merton and Irene Strommen asked the 8,165 young adolescents in their study if they wished they could talk with their parents more, less, or the same as they do now about each of the following five things: drugs, friends, school, sex, and ideas of right and wrong. They found that "young adolescents . . . are more parent-oriented than peer-oriented. They prefer being able to talk with their parents about issues that bother them. Grade five is a time of special opportunity for parents to help the young adolescent initiate conversations and learn how to communicate on a feeling level." However, the Strommens noted that interest in discussing adolescent issues with their parents steadily declines between fifth grade (58 percent) and ninth grade (37 percent).[1]

To help you take advantage of these years, read the excellent book *How to Talk So Kids Will Listen and Listen So Kids Will Talk* by Adele Faber and Elaine Mazlish. You'll find many great tips for drawing out your adolescent. We also encourage you to adopt the following three communication tips. They will also be helpful for those later teen years when your son or daughter is less likely to share his or her ideas with you.

Watch for Open Gates

Teens often want to talk to us at the most inconvenient time—when the dinner is about to burn, when we're tired and want a couple of minutes alone to regroup, late at night, right before guests are to arrive. Carter, a parent in one of our parenting seminars, shared the following story:

"Our son got home from his very first prom at 2 A.M. The evening had been super. As he sat on the side of our bed, he spilled out all the exciting details on and on until all we wanted to do was sleep! Finally we said, 'Tell us the rest in the morning!' You guessed it; the day-after conversation never happened. Two A.M. was the open gate, not the morning after. We never heard the rest of the prom details."

When our children were younger, it was easy to plan communication times—all we had to do was ask them to go out for ice cream. Not so with teens! Some of their friends might see them—and to be seen with a parent would be social suicide for a thirteen-year-old.

Start looking for open gates, and once the gate begins to open, help keep it open by comments like "Really?" "You did, huh?" "Interesting!" "Tell me more about it; I'd be interested in your point of view." Statements like these give kids a chance to really open up. Many times teens test whether or not it is safe to say what they really feel by making shocking statements. If you do not react, they can continue; if a lecture results, they close up.

Find Communication Centers

During our children's teenage years we moved into a new house. We experienced that lost feeling of not knowing where anything is or where to put the things we were unpacking. We learned that settling in is much more than arranging furniture and kitchen accessories; it's also discovering those special places that foster communication.

In this new home our den became the place where we had the best conversations; if we were sitting there, our teens would usually come and join us. Conversations just seemed to open up easier in front of the fireplace.

Stop for a moment and think about where communication flows easiest in your home. Then plan to be there frequently with a listening ear.

Find Communication Activities

Sports played an important role in building communication in our family. We learned to ski when we were in our thirties. As we shivered on a chairlift with our boys or tried to get down a scary slope, our relationships soared. The cold feet and sore muscles were worth it. So were the sore muscles from playing tennis with our sons. We slugged it out on the court and then sat together afterwards, sweaty and tired, often laughing over everything that happened. To be honest, there have also been parent-teen tennis disasters with bad calls and angry losers; but the good times outnumbered the bad times.

We are not saying that you have to become a "jock" when your children hit the adolescent years, but in our family, sports have provided a backdrop for communication and deeper sharing. Other activities may serve the same purpose: Shopping with girls, singing with musical teens, surfing the Internet or studying computer programs with computer buffs can foster more in-depth communication. Have you made your adolescents' interests yours? It takes work. Sports opened the communication gates in our home. What will open yours?

Challenge

Determine this week to listen to your kids without reacting, lecturing, or giving advice, so that you may build strong communication with them. Take some time to answer the following questions.

1. How can you give your adolescents space in your relationship?

- Physically?
- Emotionally?

2. Where does most communication take place in your home?

3. What activities do you have in common with your adolescents? Do those activities foster communication?

4. What other activities would you like to develop?

CHAPTER
7

When the Bridge Is Out

Sue, the mother of two teenager sons, shared this midnight story with the other parents in her PEP Group:

"Muffled voices drifted into my subconscious and woke me up. 'Hi, what ya doing?' 'You'll never believe it.' 'It's really cool.' 'Want to . . . ?'

"I rolled over in bed and rubbed my eyes. The time? I looked at the alarm clock; it read 12:30 A.M. Was I dreaming? It might have been a nightmare but not a dream; the voices that I still heard were outside the window next to ours, our son's window. Irritation began to escalate as I thought, *It's not fair. I'm tired! I deserve my sleep!* I stormed out of bed and into our son's room.

"Immediately I launched into a lecture on being inconsiderate, how I needed my sleep, and the inappropriateness of late night visitors. Then I noticed a rope near the window.

"'What are you going to use that rope for anyway? Rappelling out the window, by chance?' I launched into my favorite lecture on trust. Angry words having been unloaded, I retreated back to bed.

"The next morning I wondered how I could rebuild the bridge I'd burned in the early morning hours. How did I burn it? I'd hurled accusations and vented my anger."

Sue needed the good advice Dr. Ginott gives in his book *Between Parent and Teenager*. Consider these three principles:

1. Don't attack personality attributes.
2. Don't criticize character traits.
3. Deal with the situation at hand.

Dr. Ginott continues: "When things go wrong, it is not the right time to tell a teenager anything about his personality or character. When a person is drowning, it is not a good time to teach him to swim or to ask him questions or criticize his performance. It is a time to help!"[1]

We can apply all we've learned about listening, identifying feelings, and promoting conversations, but the communication bridge will still frequency sag and occasionally burn down. It is hard to face failures, especially when we're trying. But we're all human, so we can expect that we or our children will blow it.

When Parents Burn the Bridge

Back to Sue's dilemma. "Nothing could change the fact that I had blown it, but what could I do to rebuild the bridge I'd burned down the night before? The first thing I needed to do was to apologize. To my son I said, 'I was wrong to accuse you, to vent my anger at you, and not to listen. It wasn't your fault that your friends came by at 12:30 A.M. Will you forgive me?'

"Secondly, I decided to offer my son a helping hand as he was refinishing a piece of furniture to earn extra money. Stripping paint rates in my popularity book about where I put stripping unstrippable wallpaper or cleaning the oven. It was hard work, but as we were sanding we were also stripping our negative feelings, which had been the bridge burners the night before. Also, by my positive actions, I was showing my son that I was on his team.

"If I had actually caught him using that rope to rappel down the side of our house, obviously I would have taken a different course of action. Sneaking out of the house in the middle of the night is a major offense in our house."

Sue discovered that parents don't have to live with burned bridges. They can be repaired—but it's usually up to the parent to take the first step.

It's important to apologize and to do so appropriately. Resist the natural tendency to point the finger and make excuses. Using an apology as an opportunity to lecture is a mistake. (Remember in chapter 2 we talked about how we need to take the log out of our own eye!)

Instead, you need to name your fault: "I hurled insults and vented my anger on you. Will you forgive me?" Do not remind your teens what they did wrong or ask, "Now, don't you have something to say to me?"

When you are willing to apologize, then your adolescents will eventually learn to do the same.

When Teens Burn the Bridge

Adolescents often close the communication lines when they are frustrated or angry. Consider the following scene:

> Parent: "What's wrong, Maggie?"
> Maggie: "He's a creep, a first-class idiot! Why did I ever want to go out with him?"
> Parent: "You sound angry, what happened?"
> Maggie: "I don't want to talk about it, just leave me alone."

Maggie storms into her room, slams the door, turns the music up ten decibels, and stays in her room for hours. Maggie is obviously hurt, but her parent is also hurt and clueless as to how to help.

When adolescents cause the failure, often the verbal abuse ricochets and hits the parents, who are not really the cause of the anger but who just happen to be there to get the brunt of the emotion. How can parents rebuild this bridge when they weren't the ones who burned it in the first place?

Be a Forgiver

Parents need to be willing to forgive their adolescents even when not asked to. No relationship can continue without forgiveness, and parents are more equipped to begin the bridge-building process in this relationship.

One friend who has a very rocky history with her daughter told us, "I start each day with a fresh slate. I wipe away all the previous day's hurts and angry verbal attacks each morning and give my daughter the opportunity to start over again."

It hurts when your adolescents are unkind, but you must not allow your pain to damage the relationships. Once you get to the place where you can deal with your own hurts and forgive your teens, you can look at the situation more objectively.

Sometimes a note will open up the communication. Maggie's mother handled her situation by writing the following note, which she placed on Maggie's desk the next day.

> *Dear Maggie,*
>
> *You really looked nice this morning. You have a real knack for putting clothes together. I know it hurts to have someone disappoint you. I have been praying about the situation with Rob and know you'll use wisdom in handling it. I'm so thankful you are my daughter!*
>
> > *I love you,*
> > *Mom*
>
> *P.S. My ear is open if you want to talk!*

Maggie's mom communicated her trust, her love, and her desire to help, but she didn't push herself on Maggie. Her postscript let her daughter know she was available.

Perhaps you're wondering how adolescents respond to such notes and letters. Some may give you a hug and tell you they love you. Others may not mention your note, but don't be surprised if they put it away for safekeeping. The point is, don't write letters to get a response; write letters—and forgive without being asked, rub backs, drive car pools—to show your kids you love them and to be a positive parent and role model.

Live with Some Ambiguity

There are times when adolescents simply need some breathing room—not a hovering parent. If you wrote a note with every upset, your kids would soon tune you out.

Generally most parents would like to have everything neatly packaged and in order, but with teenagers it's not always possible or healthy. When adolescents wrestle with hard situations and broken relationships, you may desperately want to jump in and help; but sometimes the best way to help is by giving a little emotional space.

No one has come up with the perfect formula for relating to any other human being, much less a changing adolescent. Only God can give us wisdom to discern when to write a note and when to give space. In James 1:5, we are told, "If any of you lacks wisdom, he should ask God, who gives generously to all without finding fault, and it will be given to him."

This verse is very comforting for parents of adolescents. God never gets weary of us asking him for wisdom. He doesn't say, "Oh, here you come again. Didn't I give them wisdom last week!" His wisdom is continually available, and parents of teenagers continually need it!

When Saying No Is the Bridge Burner

From time to time all teenagers ask for parental permission when the only answer that can be given is no. A typical instance from the Green family's archives occurred when their son Brian was a young adolescent. Brian dropped the bomb one evening.

"Mom, Dad, it's okay with you if I chew, isn't it? All my friends are doing it."

A few questions revealed that Brian had already given it a try. "Brian, do you really enjoy it?" his mom questioned.

"It was cool, except I coughed a lot."

Was this conversation really happening? As Brian's parents, Sara and Rob, listed the cons, Brian spit out his list of pros: "To me it's not a moral issue. My friends are doing it, and I like it. Besides, it's fun."

The discussion continued a little longer, and then Rob said, "Brian, we realize this is something you really want to do, but as you can tell we really have a problem with chewing tobacco. Let's drop it for the time being, but for now, please don't chew. We'll research it."

Brian agreed to this temporary restriction. "Well, I won't chew if you say I can't, but I still don't see anything wrong with it."

It would be pure fiction to say that this issue ended here. For an extended time smokeless tobacco was a hot topic in their home. Sara and Rob researched the subject and presented the results of their study, but Brian still wasn't convinced.

"No, you can't chew! Issue ended," is easy to say. The issue may be ended, but so is the communication. Throughout this ordeal, Brian's parents let him express his feelings. At the same time, he valued his relationship with his parents enough not to chew—most of the time!

Situations will arise; count on it! How you handle a situation determines whether or not communication is broken.

When You Have to Say No

Here are six ways to keep communication open when you have to say no to your teens:

- Listen and be willing to identify with your adolescents' feelings. Let your children say how they feel as long as it is done in an appropriate way.
- Be patient! How much easier it would be to say "No, and that's final!" This approach may be easy, but could result in loss of communication and secrets behind parents' backs.
- Keep things light. Let humor be a guest in every discussion.
- Concentrate on the relationship. Don't allow the issue to become a "gloom cloud" that threatens to destroy your friendship with your teens.
- Proclaim a "cooling down period." If you become angry when an issue comes up, if it's not urgent, wait twenty-four hours before dealing with it.
- Don't allow yourself to get pulled into an issue right before a meal when your blood sugar and patience are both low. Offer an alternative time to discuss the issue.

Keep things in perspective: a particular situation is probably temporary. If the issue is not life-threatening (dress codes, makeup, hairstyles), ask yourself how important will it be in ten years? Then ask yourself how much more important will the relationship be in ten years?

Deal with the issue as best you can, but do all you can to preserve the relationship.

Communication Bridge Builders

Both parents and teens need to work at preventing future bridge washouts. Consider the following three principles that worked for us:

1. *Avoid "you" statements.* Statements that begin with the word "you" tend to attack others, while "I" statements reflect back on the speaker and are much safer to use. Compare the difference between these statements:

"You make me so angry!" vs. "I am so angry!"

"You don't love me!" vs. "I really feel unloved!"

2. *Avoid "why" questions.* Questions that begin with the word "why" often lead to broken bridges. For instance, "Why can't you be more considerate of me and pick up your mess in the TV room?" does not instill an attitude of cooperation. Better: "The TV room is something else. Do you think you could get it back in order?" The key is to attack the problem, not the personality.

3. *Express feelings.* We talked earlier about the importance of listening for and identifying feelings as your teens are talking to you. Equally important is the need to express your feelings and help your kids express their own feelings. Here is a simple formula that we have used for years. Simply state how you feel about a given situation. ("I feel frustrated when food and dirty dishes are left in the TV room. It is extra work for me and would be so simple if each of us would pick up after ourselves.") Then ask for their response. ("How do you feel about this?") This way you can deal with the issue at hand, and your teens are not defensive. Often the response will be, "Gee, Mom and Dad, I'm sorry I left the mess. I'll try to remember next time." The issue

has been confronted (messed-up TV room) and the relationship preserved.

When you must disagree with your teens, you could say something like this, "This may be the way you see it, but this is how I see it." Again, you are expressing your feelings without attacking the person.

When Anger Burns the Bridge

One of the greatest causes of parent-teen communication breakdown is dealing inappropriately with anger. You may know all the communication skills and are determined to use them, but then something happens to make you angry and all of your common sense goes out the window! Sound familiar? If you've never been angry at your child this section is not for you (and we would like to meet you). For most, anger is just a part of life. The question is, "How can we deal with anger in a constructive way without destroying the communication bridge?"

Learn to Be Angry

The apostle Paul told the Ephesians to "be angry but do not sin" (Eph. 4:26 RSV). For many, this may appear to be a contradiction. Anger is a frequent visitor; harsh words strain the bridge supports, and before we know it we're on opposite sides of the crevice with no way to cross over. Since anger is often around, how can we deal with anger without sinning?

Solomon put it this way: "A fool gives full vent to his anger, but a wise man keeps himself under control." What is the balance? How can we handle our anger and train our teens to handle theirs in an appropriate way?

Start by realizing that anger is a secondary reaction to fear or frustration. It gives you that extra adrenaline to get out of harm's way. Suppose your sixteen-year-old has taken the family car to run some errands. The time goes by and he is late. What is your response? Perhaps you're fearful that your inexperienced driver has been in an accident. Then after a few minutes you hear the car pull into the driveway. What happens to your fear? It's instantly transformed into anger—which you then release on your new driver!

By understanding why you are angry, you will be able to discern whether your anger is legitimate or not.

The Anger Ladder

Knowing how to handle anger effectively is something we can learn. The more mature a person is, the more maturely he or she will handle his or her anger. However, some adults have never learned how to handle anger and are poor role models for their teens, yet they expect their teens to handle anger in an appropriate way or even not to express anger at all.

In his book *How to Really Love Your Teenager*, Dr. Ross Campbell deals with different ways of handling anger.[2] Picture a ladder with six levels. Each level represents a way to handle anger. Level 1 is the worst or least effective way to handle anger and number 6 is the best or most appropriate way. The goal is to move up the ladder as we learn better ways of dealing with our angry feelings.

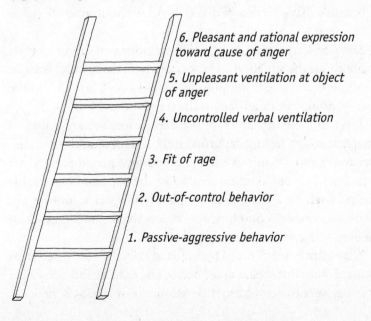

6. Pleasant and rational expression toward cause of anger

5. Unpleasant ventilation at object of anger

4. Uncontrolled verbal ventilation

3. Fit of rage

2. Out-of-control behavior

1. Passive-aggressive behavior

The anger ladder is a great concept to share with your adolescent, but share it after everyone has calmed down. Consider the following example:

It had been a fun tennis match until the last point. Hank won that point and told his brother, Chris, that he could have easily gotten the ball that he missed. Chris didn't appreciate this remark from his younger brother and began to criticize Hank's game. Tempers flared, and the cold war escalated. Hank will be our example as we go through the six levels and see how he could have reacted.

Level 1: Passive-aggressive behavior (won't talk, but gets even). Hank could have hidden his anger toward Chris, then later broken Chris's new stereo or "misplaced" Chris's tennis racket.

Level 2: Out-of-control behavior (hits people and breaks things). Hank could have gone into a fit of rage and thrown down his tennis racket, stomped on it until it broke, and slugged Chris or maybe even hit an innocent bystander.

Level 3: Fit of rage (desires to "hurt" someone by screaming or yelling). Hank could have yelled and screamed at Chris, trying to hurt him verbally. He may have even verbally attacked others.

Level 4: Uncontrolled verbal ventilation (yells and screams). Hank could have lacked verbal control without attempting to hurt anyone.

Level 5: Unpleasant ventilation at object of anger (speaks harshly about the situation). Hank could have dealt with his anger by yelling or crying, confining his remarks to Chris and to the issue: "I do not want advice on the tennis court!"

Level 6: Pleasant and rational expression toward cause of anger (expresses feelings appropriately). Hank could have said, "I'm angry and I don't like it when you give me advice!" Later Hank and Chris could rationally discuss the issue and make some decision such as, "Next time we play tennis, let's confine our remarks to honest compliments. When we're practicing drills together, you can give me tips and advice."

What actually happened? Hank reacted at level 4—he yelled at his brother. Rather than being upset because he didn't handle his anger better, his parents were pleased that he was not at level 1, 2, or 3.

Passive-aggressive behavior (level 1) may be the least obvious, but it is the most destructive and the least appropriate way to handle anger. Violent behavior (levels 2 and 3) is obviously inappropriate, although the expression of anger is the right step. Verbally abusive behavior (levels 4 and 5) misses the mark, although it shows more self-control than previous levels. Peaceful confrontational behavior (level 6) deals with the anger without succumbing to it.

Dr. Campbell states, "Resolving the issue means for both parties to rationally and logically examine the issue, discuss it, understand it from both points of view, and to come to an agreement on what to do about it. This takes a great deal of maturity on both sides. Few people ever come to this point of maturity in their lives."

Dr. Campbell challenges parents to be good examples in expressing their own anger and to expect anger to be frequent when teens are present in the home. "Instead of forbidding our teens from becoming angry or overreacting to their anger, we need to meet them where they are in handling their anger and train them from there. Our goal for ourselves and our teens is verbal expression of anger."[3]

How to Climb the Ladder

Several days after the tennis saga, Hank, Chris, and their parents sat down and talked about anger levels. Together they identified Hank's present level and helped him to set a higher goal for the next time he was angry.

To help you advance to higher, more productive levels of anger, review the six levels of anger with your teens. This works best during a calm time. Discuss typical reactions and more appropriate ones. Maybe your teens will say something like, "I'm at level 4. Maybe I can move up a notch."

The best time to help your kids learn how to process anger appropriately is when they are upset with someone besides you. When adolescents are angry and upset, you need to let them talk without lecturing about how wrong it is to hate or express anger inappropriately. They need someone to listen to them, not to solve everything for them. After their strong feelings diminish, you can help them evaluate how they are handling their anger.

Are we saying that it is okay for your teens to hate? No, but if you try to monitor every fit of anger and correct every spoken word, sooner or later, you will find your teens have tuned you out. You want to help them handle their anger effectively, not to bury it or deny it.

To Sum It Up

Burned bridges—whether burned by a parent, a teen, a refusal, or a fit of rage—don't have to remain a disaster. Reconstruction can start today, and it can start with you. You can begin by forgiving and then asking for forgiveness. You can bridge that crevice between you and your teens through common communication activities, by writing a note, or by giving space. You can patiently listen for feelings and resist the role of being a judge. Any issue, light or heavy, is not really as important as the relationship. Again, ask yourself, "Will this problem be important in ten years? Will my relationship with my son or daughter be important then?" The obvious answer will help you regain your perspective.

Challenge

1. Think of a time that you have blown it. How could you have responded differently?

2. This week practice using the feelings formula: "Let me tell you how I feel. . . . Now tell me how you feel."

3. Go over the anger ladder with your adolescents or as a family.

- Discuss appropriate ways of handling anger.
- Let each person identify where he or she generally is on the ladder.

4. Agree to work together to move up a rung on the ladder.

CHAPTER
8

Good Housekeeping or Groady to the Max?

When I get my room just the way I want it my mom makes me clean it up!

Thirteen-year-old girl

How many times have you found yourself in a major blowup over a relatively minor issue? Before you know it, you're caught in a struggle you wished you had allowed to pass by. Or maybe you have difficulty deciding if something is really a major or a minor.

Recently as we were launching a MOM's & DAD's Support Group on a U.S. army base, one dad (who was a drill sergeant) spoke up. "My son is totally disrespectful. He is irresponsible, lazy, and disobedient."

As we began to ask a few questions, we discovered the major issue in this parent-adolescent tug-of-war was the condition of his son's room. "I tell him he is a slob—to get his room organized, to pick up his clothes, and make up his bed, and he just looks at me and says, 'Why? What's the big deal? I like it this way. It's my room.'"

"The big deal," his wife interjected, "is that the tension over the condition of his son's room is wrecking his relationship with his son!"

"What relationship?" this dad continued. "We never have just a normal conversation. But respect is a major to me, and if he doesn't keep his room the way I want him to, he is being disrespectful. The men in my company wouldn't dare speak to me like my son does, and when I tell them to jump, their only reply is, 'How high, sir?'"

Tactfully, we tried to help this drill-sergeant dad understand that relating to his adolescent son the way he relates to his army troops will not be helpful to either him or his son. Plus, it doesn't work! Giving the orders of the day concerning rooms causes more problems than it solves.

Another parent in the group spoke up. "I don't like the condition of my daughter's room, but frankly, I've got bigger hills to die on. I just shut the door! But when it comes to how my daughter dresses—it may not be major, but who wants your kid to go out looking like a hooker? How do you decide what are the issues worth fighting for?"

Consider another parenting dilemma. Julie came home from the school trip with double-pierced ears. Her mother exploded. She was furious, shocked, and hurt that her thirteen-year-old daughter would do this behind her back. After the big explosion, Julie's mom gave her two alternatives: let the second hole in her ears disappear or give up her own private phone she had just gotten for her birthday. With a big smile she surrendered her phone!

Julie's mother described the situation. "Not only does she still have those double-pierced ears, but now I spend all my time answering her phone calls and hollering up the stairs. Of course she can't hear me because her door is closed, and her CD player is blaring away. I'm asking myself, who is being punished? Are two little holes in her ears major enough to allow so much tension in our relationship?"

"Whatever happened to good old black and white? It's all gray. Everything is gray!" Janice said. "When the kids were younger, right was right, wrong was wrong. Black was black and white, white. But once my kids hit the adolescent years, the whole world turned gray. So many decisions I have to make seemed to fall in that gray area. How important are hairstyles, academics, music, and choice of friends? Is it really wrong to be grungy to the max?"

Can you relate to these parents? With so many controversial areas, you can't make a major issue out of everything. You can only win so many battles, so you must choose which battles are important enough to fight.

Majors and Minors

If you asked your adolescents, "What five issues do you think are most important to your parents?" what would they answer? Would these issues match your own top-five list? Each parent's list will be a little different, but the goal is to decide what is most important to you. Our best advice is to determine what the major issues are and then save your emotional energy for these important issues.

During the adolescent years, the majors in our family had more to do with attitudes—respect, honesty, openness, willingness to buck peer pressure and at times to stand alone. Yet as our boys entered the teen years, daily they heard us raising issues like clothes, rooms, music, grooming, hairstyles, and neatness!

It's not that the minors are not issues to be dealt with, but too often minor issues become major irritations. If you want to do more than just survive the adolescent years, you need to major on the majors and minor on the minors. We learned we had to flex in those areas that were not moral issues like pierced ears and phone time and stand firm in those that were moral issues like lying or stealing. So, when faced with a situation, we would ask ourselves, "Is this really a moral issue or just our personal preference?"

To help determine if an issue is a major or a minor, practice asking yourself the question, "Is it a moral issue?" For instance, a parent's aversion to hairstyles and modes of dress may stem from their own opinions and biases, and so parents and teens can probably work out a compromise. With moral issues, however, there should be no compromise.

Another helpful question is, "What difference will it make in light of eternity?" It's amazing how this question gives perspective. While we still have to live with the minors, we need to keep them from becoming major irritations like the drill-sergeant dad's experience. Let's consider several minor areas, which tend to cause parent-teen tug-of-wars.

Rooms or Tombs

Is it true that children can be born neat? If you have such a child, skip this section. More likely you can identify with the parent who said, "I've tried everything from punishment to bribes, but my son's room would still turn a respectable rat's stomach." Consider the following parent-teen dialogue:

Parent: "How would you describe your room?"

Teen: "But I picked up my clothes!"

Parent: "How do you like your room?"

Teen: "Cool! Fantastic!"

Parent: "I mean the condition of it. How you keep it."

Teen: "Oh, it's a mess, but that's why it's cool and fantastic!"

One teen described her ideal room this way: "It's a place that is all yours—where you can shut the door and be alone with your own thoughts. Sometimes my thoughts are jumbled and so my room is too. Sometimes an unmade bed is part of the picture. That's because a cozy nest of blankets and a pillow feels good when you study and eat pretzels on the bed."

Different Perspectives

It's obvious that parents and adolescents view rooms from two completely different perspectives. If you aspire to a *House Beautiful* home, then let us give a word of warning. Little children love for the parent to "redo" their room with cute Winnie-the-Pooh wallpaper, and preteens may still enjoy redecorating with you, but when they hit the adolescent years, you need to consider things from the teenagers' perspective.

One parent said, "Our son chose to decorate his room in what can only be termed as 'Early Grotesque.' He has red walls, a red carpet, black drapes, and a fake animal skin spread. Mobiles attack you, posters affront you, anything that takes his fancy we allow. Know why? It's his room, and he's the one who has to live with it.

Because it is his own, we have found he would just as soon have friends over as go out, and that means less worry for us. I overheard one kid say, 'Wow! Your parents are great. I wish mine would let me fix my room up!' When you give a little, you get a lot!"

Tips for Trying

What can you do to reach a truce with your adolescents? Start by asking yourself, "Is the state of affairs in my adolescents' rooms a major or a minor?" Our favorite approach is simply to put the responsibility for your teenagers' rooms in their Birthday Boxes. Let it be their domain. Interfere only if the other alternative is calling the Center for Disease Control. While this approach works for the more laid-back parent, if you can't live with the condition of your kids' rooms, try some of the following four suggestions.

1. Offer a reward.

Make your kids' allowance based on the condition of their rooms. This will work for a short time, but you need to be disciplined because what isn't inspected will not be accomplished.

One parent gave the following challenge to her twelve-year-old daughter, who desperately wanted contact lenses: "When you keep your room neat for one month, you have proven you are responsible and old enough for contact lenses."

If you're concerned you might be bribing your child, rest easy. We all work for positive reinforcement!

2. Try humor.

Hang a sign by the phone that says on one side, "As I today through your room went walking, I saw that it was O.K. for phone talking." On the other side say: "Today your room did not pass— so no phoning today—Alas! Alas!" Or put a note on the towel, "Hello, I don't like being on the cold floor, please take me back to the bathroom and hang me up. Thanks! Your loving towel."

3. Negotiate.

One smart parent in a PEP Group took the following approach: "Arnold, what can I do to make your room work for you?"

Since Arnold didn't like his present desk (which went great with the room decor), he studied on the bed, with messy results. The first thing he wanted was a drafting board desk. With this one change, his study habits changed. After all, it's harder to fall asleep at a drafting board than on a bed! Also, this smart parent added shelves to the son's closet and made a place for his hiking boots, sleeping bag, and other camping gear and sports equipment.

Did it make a difference? "With things more organized," this parent reported to the PEP Group, "Arnold is doing a much better job of keeping his room clean. And I'm not continually hassling him about his room."

4. If nothing works, close the door.

Sometimes closing the door is the best approach unless we want to make a clean room a major issue, which may result in a major battle. Let us assure you, almost everyone has those "closed door days" too. Whatever you do, concentrate on maintaining the relationship—it's far more important than a messy bedroom!

Grooming

How is a parent to motivate adolescents to comb their hair, brush their teeth, and be respectably clean? These are not called the grunge years for nothing! One answer is to wait. In a matter of months they will probably be obsessed with what they are now trying to avoid.

One friend commented, "I still cannot believe it has happened! Six months ago it took a state of war to get my daughter to wash her hair. She seemed not even to notice the grease that looked ready to drip onto her collar.

"Now she has done a total flip-flop! Last night she washed her hair without being asked and rolled it in curlers. This morning she wet her brush, combed out some of the curls, and then recurled them with the curling iron! Now I'm not sure which is better, the greasies or the hair obsession. At least with the greasies she didn't monopolize the bathroom!"

A frequent controversy between parents and young adolescent girls is makeup. Preteens see makeup as a symbol of maturity. They use an eyebrow pencil and mascara as if they were dressing for Halloween. Sometimes this is just a lack of skill; other times it's deliberate.

One mother in a PEP Group shared her experience: "When my daughters were eleven and twelve, they became very interested in makeup. This seemed too young to me, but rather than allow this to become a 'major,' I agreed to teach them how to use makeup to achieve a natural look. I complimented them when they were able to apply a little eye shadow expertly.

"But would you believe it? Before long they lost interest. Now that they're older, I'm the one who asks them to put a dab of color on their cheeks."

Often teaching preteens to use makeup properly will solve problems that might develop later. You might want to suggest getting some free professional cosmetic advice from the cosmetic counter of a local department store. Most analysts will suggest proper makeup to go with skin tones and will also show your adolescent how to apply makeup properly.

Fads Are for Driving Parents Wild!

What were the fads when you were a teenager? Are today's styles really any worse than those of other generations? Recently in a local mall we observed the following:

1. Very baggy pants—at least five sizes too large!
2. Multiple earrings (and not just in the ear!)
3. Various colors of hair
4. Black, black, and more black
5. Combat boots
6. Weird-colored lipstick and nail polish

While teenage fads usually aren't majors, we do suggest avoiding extremes of being too lax or too strict. The parents of one teen would not let their daughter cut her hair or wear pants because of religious convictions. Each morning this teenager went to her friend's house before school and changed from her skirt into her jeans that she hid there. Each week she snipped off a few locks of hair, so gradually her hair got shorter and shorter.

One parent took the opposite approach. "Unless the kid shows a tendency to go berserk or way overboard," she advised, "let them choose for themselves. They will make mistakes, but at least they cannot say, 'My parents made me wear this junk.'"

We love what a youth pastor told a PEP parenting group: "If you can cut if off, wash it out, or grow it out, don't sweat it! I'm convinced that if you give a little on dress and hair, your adolescent will be more apt to respond positively in those areas that are really important."

Another mom told us that in her daughter Ginny's early teen years, Ginny bought all her clothes on the street near a local university where she could find clothes to fit her taste. One day Ginny joined her mother for a luncheon at a very exclusive private club. All the women and their daughters were dressed conservatively.

Our friend told us later, "The only way to describe Ginny's garb was that she looked like a gypsy!"

Did this bother our friend? Would it bother you? When our friend asked herself why she was upset, she had to admit, "It's my pride. I was scared by that age-old worry, 'What will other people think of my daughter?'"

The better question, she knew, was, Is this a moral issue? "No, it isn't," she decided.

This guideline works for most parents, except in the rare instances when a young person's dress really hurts the teen or someone else. Susan told the women in her PEP Group of just such an experience. Her daughter, Wendy, began to show some interest in clothes when she was eleven, but her taste left much to be desired, so Susan was constantly advising her to change a blouse or skirt so her outfit would match.

Finally Wendy erupted. "I've had enough of your taste, Mom," she asserted. "I want to choose my own clothes."

In exasperation, Susan relented. Wendy went to school with her clothes mismatched and wrinkled and her hair disheveled. Her mom bit her tongue and let her go. After two weeks, Wendy's teacher called and asked her mom to come in for a consultation. As soon as Susan sat down, the teacher observed,

"You're so nicely dressed. Why doesn't Wendy dress nicely?" The teacher went on to explain that Wendy alienated herself from the other kids by dressing so oddly. That did it. Susan told Wendy, "You may call the shots on your dress only when you begin to show the ability to dress neatly."

According to Susan, here's the regime that she instituted: "First, I got her a short hairstyle that required no talent to keep, only that she had to comb her hair! Wendy could pick her clothes in the morning but I had to approve them before she left for school. I agreed to iron for her for one more year, but she was to iron occasionally and take over after that. After three years, this is still a concern, but Wendy has shown much improvement. She'll never be a fashion designer, but she is learning to use taste in her preferences."

Music: Bach or Rock

As the Miller family moved into the teenage years, it became obvious that their blooming adolescents had an interest in new forms of music. This is their story:

"When our kids began to get into the music scene, a song from my own teenage years, 'Help, I Need Somebody,' expressed my feeling of inadequacy. So I began to poll other parents with older teens who seemed to be doing great. (Never overlook the potential gold mine of information and experience from other families who are a few years farther down the road than you are.)

"After gathering information, Frank and I came up with the following guidelines for our children in the early teen years. As our adolescents matured and became older, we gave them more freedom in choosing their own music."

The Millers' music guidelines at ages eleven to thirteen were as follows:

1. Let parents listen to your new tapes and CDs. Listen to and talk about any concerns parents might have about choice of music.
2. Before school, play music the whole family likes.
3. After school no rock music until homework is completed or until you have studied for at least an hour.

4. No loud rock music an hour before bedtime.

5. When others are around and protest, use earphones.

6. On Sunday let rock rest.

These music guidelines worked much of the time. With one kid, they actually wrote out a music contract, which he signed. Spelling it out aided enforcement.

Music Contract Between Carl and Parents

I hereby agree to the following:

  1. Before school I will play only Christian music.

  2. After school I may play my choice of music after completing one hour of homework.

  3. After 8:00 P.M. I will play Christian music.

  4. After my younger brother is in bed, I will use earphones.

  5. At 9:30 P.M. all music will be off.

  6. On Sunday I will play only Christian music.

If this contract is broken, I agree to the following:

First offense: No radio or recorder for 24 hours.

Second offense: No radio or recorder for 48 hours.

Third offense: No radio or recorder for 96 hours.

Signed_____

Date_____

A Word of Caution!

This worked for the Millers, but one dad who read about this contract said his son's response would have been, "Dad, I'd listen to elevator music all day before I'd sign that!" We would not recommend using this approach with older adolescents or with kids who are already choosing their own music.

Monitor Different Music Groups

Since most adolescents find it hard to accept a parent's assessment that a group is inappropriate, we polled a group of teenagers and here is their advice:

"Listen to the lyrics with your children. What do the lyrics say? Talk about them together. Don't just limit this exercise to rock music. Country music or easy listening music may be more appealing to adults, but some of the lyrics are really immoral. And don't overlook music videos. Take the same approach for evaluating them."

Over the years at our house, we monitored the different music groups that our kids listened to. From time to time we sat down with our adolescents, listened to their music, and talked about the lyrics. Together we evaluated the message.

When one of our sons was fourteen and had shown some discrimination, we agreed to let him basically make his own choices. Did he disappoint his parents? No, he actually became more selective in his music choices. Another son, who at thirteen needed firm guidelines for music, had established good values by fifteen.

We are not saying that music is never a problem to be dealt with. We are saying that in our experience, by giving in a little, we achieved a good balance, avoided war, and gained a lot of working capital. We bought tapes and records for our teens that we liked, but we let them support their own rock habit.

Giving a little in this area can help avoid rebellion in other areas like drugs, drinking, and premarital sex. Most adolescents have a desire to control their own lives, and sometimes we strip them of this control just when they most yearn for it—try to be flexible with your young adolescents.

By the way, our son who was most into rock music, now, years later, chooses to listen to classical music and seldom watches television!

Now It's Your Turn

It's great to read what others have done in similar experiences, but the final decision as to which areas are minor and which are major in your family is yours. Don't make these decisions lightly. You might want to discuss some of the issues with your spouse, since you will have to agree on how to handle them. Don't wait until the problems arise. If you do, you'll be caught in the emotion of the moment.

"I Never Promised You a Rose Garden" could be the theme song for both parents and teenagers. Both must somehow cope with the teens' struggles through dramatic physical changes, identity formation, feelings of inferiority, the need to conform, and wild emotional upheavals. Your teens do not need your hassling them over minor issues. Trusting God with their lives, withstanding peer pressure, developing positive attitudes, and learning decision-making skills are the more important issues of life. Save your ammunition for the important battles yet to come. Deal with the minors without making them major issues, then you'll have the energy to tackle the majors in life.

Challenge

1. List five areas that you feel are (or should be) minor issues.

2. Relate one situation when you created a major battle over a minor issue.

3. What minor area is creating tension in your home right now?

4. What can you do to reduce friction in this area this week?

CHAPTER
9

Majoring on the Majors

We were the keynote speakers at a weeklong family conference. While most of our keynote addresses were to the parents, on this evening the teenagers were also part of our audience. But from the expressions on their faces, we could sense that they would rather be anywhere else!

First, we thanked the teenagers for dragging their parents to this meeting despite their uncooperative attitudes. A few chuckles encouraged us to continue. Then we introduced the topic of majors and minors. "What are the things your parents major on?" we asked. Before we knew it, we had filled a chalkboard with everything from writing thank-yous to eating breakfast.

Then we asked the parents what things their teenagers considered majors. It was obvious these parents and teenagers didn't live on the same planet! No wonder they seemed at cross-purposes.

Next we did something that at the time seemed risky. We asked individual families to dialogue together on what should be the majors and minors in their home and to do some negotiating. But before deciding if an issue was major or minor we encouraged them to ask the two questions we discussed in the last chapter:

Is it a moral issue?
What difference will it make in ten years? In light of eternity?

To our amazement, as we looked around the room, parents and teens were actually talking with each other! Later, several parents told us this evening was the highlight of the whole week.

Years later we continued to get good feedback. Some of the families for the first time got on the same page regarding what their majors and minors should be.

Such cooperation in families with adolescents usually doesn't happen spontaneously. Instead, parents may set goals for their adolescents without consulting them, often resulting in goals the teens wouldn't choose. As a parent, goal setting for your children frequently begins with the moment you first hold your babies in the hospital and ask yourself, "What is this tiny infant's future?" While such goal setting is impromptu, these goals are often firmly set in parents' minds.

Is it realistic to set goals for another person? Only if you want to set yourself up for total frustration. A goal is something you have the power to achieve—in other words, your goals should require only you to make the effort. For example, you can set a goal for yourself of getting up at six o'clock each morning; and if you want to achieve this goal badly enough, you can do it. However, if you set a goal for your teen to get up at six o'clock each morning, there is ultimately little you can do to make sure the goal is met. You can only alter and affect your own attitudes and actions. In other words, you can set a goal to be a positive role model for your teenagers, but you can't set a goal to have them respond to your efforts.

It is much more realistic to talk about our desires for our children—what we would like to see happen in their lives. Expressing our desires, instead of imposing goals, releases them from outside pressure while reinforcing personal responsibility. Expressing desires also demonstrates your confidence in and love for your kids.

In the last chapter we looked at some of the minors that can become major irritations. In this chapter we will look at areas of major concern—moral issues that do make a difference in light of eternity—like resisting peer pressure to drink, take drugs, experiment with sex, and so on; learning better relational and decision-making skills; internalizing value systems and taking ownership for spiritual growth.

In each of these areas we will talk about real situations that other parents have faced and offer some tips for dealing with potential problems. We give no definite answers, just approaches to encourage you to major on the majors creatively.

Learning to Resist Negative Peer Pressure

Many teens will admit that their greatest struggle is with negative peer pressure. What teen wants to antagonize his or her peers? Or to be different? One of the seven intuitive goals the Strommens identified was "the broadening of one's social base by having learned to make friends and maintain them."[1]

Dr. Bruce Narramore in *Adolescence Is Not an Illness* writes, "Our offspring's urge to conform usually sharpens during the preteen and early teenage years. Their susceptibility to peer pressure then peaks around middle adolescence, and begins a gradual decline. In spite of the potentially negative influence of peer pressure, the process behind it is entirely natural and God-given. Our teenagers are susceptible to their friends' influence because they are in the process of weaning themselves from us and learning to think for themselves. In a sense, our teenagers are going from one form of dependency, parental, to another form of dependency, peer, on their way to constructive self-reliance."[2]

Adolescent psychologists say this is normal and that it too shall pass away. But when it seems to be the all-pervading influence in your teen's life, it is scary. Consider these situations:

Pressure in Girl-Boy Relationships

One young teen received the following letter from a friend, who also happened to be his girlfriend's brother, encouraging him to "get with it."

Dear Paul,

If I had a girlfriend I would not let this happen! You are not getting anywhere (holding hands, kissing, etc.). Get that shyness away when you are around my sister.

I say this because it seems that when you are around other girls, you're not at all shy! Could you tell me why? Well, okay, it's not all your fault. I have told her off too. If I were my sister, I would have dropped you long ago but don't worry, she won't. Here are some tips for you.

1. *Hold hands*
2. *Kiss*
3. *Hug (openly)*
4. *Talk to each other*

Your friend,
John

PS: Don't kill me!

As teens grow older the pressure in boy-girl relationships gets stronger. Dealing with a note like the above is simple in comparison with being in a group where most of the other couples are already sleeping together. How can you help kids with this kind of peer pressure?

The sooner you start, the better! Even at eleven or twelve is not too soon! One tool we used to help our sons deal with peer pressure was the book *Dare to Be Different* by Fred Hartley. (The book is no longer in print, but it may be available in your church library. A great book that warns older teen girls against the problems of promiscuous sex is *Just Like Ice Cream* by Lissa Hall Johnson [Tyndale, 1995].) Dave took each of our young adolescents out to breakfast one morning a week for six weeks and discussed the book with each of them.

As awkward as it may be, talking with your adolescents about the pressure to become sexually active can open the communication lines and help them decide now what their own standards will be. Teens can survive peer pressure much better when they know what they believe and have decided beforehand on their standards of action. However, even with this advance preparation, they will at times still be influenced by their peers. If as parents you are majoring on the majors, you can realize that you are building for the future and not expecting perfection today.

Pressure to Drink

"My friends won't come," Ruth protested to her mother. "The party won't be any fun. Anyway, if they knew I wasn't going to have anything to drink, they'd bring their own."

Corrie, Ruth's mother, stood firm in her decision, but she allowed Ruth to have the party. Corrie went all out on the food and even bought near beer, a nonalcoholic version of the brew.

"Oh, Mom!" Ruth shrieked when her mother showed her the bottles. "That's worse than Kool-Aid!"

The night of the party, Ruth's father stood beside the bushes at the door to their house. When the first guest arrived, toting a cooler, he asked, "Son, what do you have in the cooler? Could I have a look inside?"

"Oh, it's just some extra ice and pop."

"Well, we've got plenty inside. Why don't you leave your cooler in the car."

That scenario was repeated over and over again.

The next day Ruth told her parents, "The party was a complete disaster! How could you and Dad do this to me?"

Later that night Corrie and her husband, Bill, evaluated the party fiasco and came up with these conclusions:

1. Our daughter hates us and is socially ruined.
2. We have two cases of untouched near beer.
3. We have prevented a drinking party.

On top of this, Bill was covered with mosquito bites. But what would have happened if there had been liquor at the party? The possibilities were too scary to think about, the parents decided.

"We'll take a disaster any day," they agreed. Corrie did, however, regret the near beer. "It's just an older version of candy cigarettes," she said. "The kids knew it was a foolish substitute."

A year later, that disastrous party had almost been forgotten. Ruth still had many friends, but she had found other ways to entertain them, such as riding in her family's new motorboat. Her father also drove her and eleven of her friends in a van for twelve hours to a youth congress in Washington, D.C.

What can you do to offset peer pressure to drink? Here are three tips:

First, get involved. Bill and Corrie say they would have preferred ten days of forced labor to that party, but the experience did help direct their daughter in another direction.

Second, check on the parties to which your teens are invited. When our boys were in their early teen years, we called the parents before we let them attend a party at a friend's home. "Will there be an adult chaperone?" we always asked. "Will drinks be served or allowed?"

When one mother responded, "Oh, no, I won't be home," we didn't let our son attend. We've heard too many stories about parties that were held when parents were away for the evening or out of town.

Third, encourage your teen to get involved in local organizations that discourage drinking. One mom told us how her son, Kurt, and his friends decided to do something positive to counteract the alcohol problem in high school. They heard about an "anti-drinking" club, which had become inactive but had been a positive influence, so they decided to form a new one. The track coach agreed to be the sponsor, and he and the boys attended some training conferences and began to bring speakers to the school. Soon the club had thirty members.

One project their club chose to sponsor was an After Prom Party, which kids could attend without the pressure to drink. A couple of weeks before the prom, they placed a wrecked car in front of the school with a sign that read "Think before you drink."

Some youths have actually made an agreement with their parents that if they are ever in a situation where they do not have a safe ride home, they will call their parents. Their parents agreed to pick them up and to discuss the issue at a later time.

Such an agreement can build trust between parents and teens. The teen knows that Mom and/or Dad will not explode and overreact. Parents know their teens will not get in a car with a drinking driver, even if their son or daughter is a victim of peer pressure and has been drinking too. Both sides know the issue will be discussed and resolved at an appropriate time.

Pressure to Take Drugs

One afternoon a professional counselor received a call from the emergency room of a local hospital. "Your son has overdosed on drugs. Could you come immediately?" said the voice on the other end of the line.

The counselor, who often worked with adolescents, had been worried about his middle son ever since his grades began slipping a year earlier. Lately, he had suspected the boy was taking drugs. *Why didn't I confront him with my suspicions?* he wondered as he walked into the hospital. Fortunately, the doctors soon assured him that his son was okay.

Later, when he saw the teenager, the boy admitted, "Gee, Dad, this is the worst thing I've ever done to you and Mom. But I'm glad it happened. I won't ever do it again."

Even with the boy's promise, we would be naive to assume the next months were easy for these parents. As a counselor, the father knew how many teens make such promises and still end up as addicts. These parents could have been consumed with guilt, but their comments to us hold wisdom for all parents.

"In our work," he said, "we have learned that you can't assume responsibility for other people's decisions. Our son is the one who decided to try drugs, not us. We tried not to dwell on the past, forever wondering how it could have happened. Instead, we looked to the future and asked ourselves how we could help him turn things around.

"When he came home from the hospital, we did all we could to structure his environment. We had rules, and he had to abide by them. We were the parents, and we did assert our authority. But because we did not carry the guilt for his unwise choices, we were not paralyzed by a sense of failure or consumed with guilt. We were free to help him."

With professional counseling this teenager lived up to his promise. His grades went back up, he graduated from high school, and he is now doing extremely well in college.

No matter how dark the situation looks, parents need to focus on the future, as this couple did, not on the past. "Where do we go from here?" is the proper question, not "How did this happen?"

Drugs are not a fad that will soon go out of style or be successfully controlled by the law. Wise parents will arm themselves with valid information.

Art Linkletter, whose youngest daughter died when she jumped out of a building during an LSD trip, gives this advice:

"You can't watch your children twenty-four hours a day. You can try to build a relationship with the child that will form a protective barrier between him and the drug menace. I'm not saying you will succeed; in spite of your best efforts, you may fail. But you will know you've tried—and believe me, this knowledge in itself may save your own sanity."[3]

Linkletter goes on to encourage parents to spend more time with their kids. Be sure to talk and to listen, he advises. "They need to know that you are interested in them, that you trust them, expect the best of them. But don't be complacent, assuming that everything's all right," he adds.[4]

Many psychologists see self-esteem as a contributing factor to drug addiction. "Most researchers in the field—even those who disagree about other matters of causation and treatment—agree that low self-regard is a crucial factor in addiction," say Dr. Harvey Milkman, associate professor of psychology at Metropolitan State College in Denver, and Dr. Stanley Sunderwirth, professor of chemistry and vice-president for academic affairs at the same college. "One way of coping with feelings of worthlessness is to immerse oneself in mood altering behavior."[5]

In addition to lack of self-esteem, Informed Families of Dade County, Inc. (Miami, Fla.), gives these other related root causes of drug abuse:

1. Lack of support systems
2. Unclear values
3. Lack of decision-making coping skills
4. Inability to set and reach goals
5. No clearly defined belief system
6. Lack of real world success experience
7. Lack of positive role models
8. Emphasis on accumulation of things; de-emphasis on healthy interpersonal relationships

Milkman and Sunderwirth also point out that the stigma of being diagnosed as a drug user further decreases the adolescent's sense of self-worth and pushes him or her more firmly into a pattern of socially unacceptable behavior. Frequently this downward spiral results in hospitalization. Research has shown that sixty to eighty percent of all addicts who attempt abstinence fail within six months.

If your teen does develop a drug addiction, you need to maintain a loving relationship with your child instead of being petrified by these statistics. One dad understood this concept. After picking up his son at the police station, an officer told the father, "He's your problem now."

"No, he's not my problem," the dad replied. "He's my son and I love him." That dad was on the right track. He recognized his son's problem and, therefore, sought counseling for the boy, but he continued to love his son unconditionally.

In his book *My Child on Drugs?* Linkletter gives the following signs and signals of drug use:

1. Lack of appetite, especially in a teenage boy
2. Short attention span
3. Slothfulness or lethargy
4. Drowsiness

5. Drunken appearance
6. Loss of memory
7. Impaired judgment
8. Staying away from home for unexplained lengths of time

"A good rule," he adds, "is to be suspicious of any sudden change that is completely out of character for the individual."[6] He also encourages parents to get to know their child's friends, to set loving limits, and to get professional help—before their child becomes another statistic.

(If you would like to read more about teen drug abuse, we particularly recommend two books: *My Child on Drugs?* by Art Linkletter and George Gallup, Jr., and *Tough Love* by Pauline Neff.)

As you help your preteens work through these major pressures in the years ahead, remember that today's giant redwood was once a little nut that held its ground.

Other Peer Related Situations

Assorted other situations are peer related. When adolescents are deceptive and slip behind their parents' back, often it's at the urging of a peer. Quite a few parents experience middle-of-the-night traumas when they wake up and find their teens have sneaked out of the house. Sometimes teens get caught by the parent or, even worse, by the police.

Let the Good Times "Roll"!

Judy slipped out of the house the first time one night when her best friend, Susie, was spending the night. Their plan? To "roll" (or "T.P.") a yard. One might define "rolling" as a form of art in which trees and mailboxes are decorated with toilet paper. The girls returned without Judy's parents seeing them.

The next time Judy tried this caper, she was not so lucky. She and some friends decided to drive to an old house everyone said was haunted. After they arrived, one boy said, "We need a souvenir. Why don't we take the mailbox? Bet witches don't get any mail."

Everyone agreed, and they began to pull and tug on the mailbox. No one saw the blue lights of the police car when it approached.

The four teens had been looking for excitement but not a ride in the patrol car to the juvenile detention center or being locked in cells. Two long hours later, Judy and her friends were released to their parents. "Honestly, we didn't know anyone lived in that house," Judy told her parents as they drove home. "We just wanted to have fun. I'm sorry. I'll never, ever, slip out again."

Judy's parents managed to remain calm and simply said, "We're glad you're okay and not hurt. We'll discuss it in the morning and work out the consequences."

The next morning the parents of the four teens met together. First, they made sure all the facts were correct. Yes, the house was known as the haunted house, as the teens had claimed. Yes, lots of kids had vandalized it, but that was no excuse. An old woman lived in the house, and her life had been made very unpleasant by all of the pranks.

Together the parents agreed upon the teens' punishment. All four teens would apologize to the woman and then spend the next Saturday mowing her yard and helping her with other housework.

Did the teens learn their lesson? Yes. Did they ever slip out again at night? We don't think so.

These parents adopted the advice in Gilbert and Sullivan's famous *Mikado*, "Let the punishment fit the crime."

But I Hate Her!

Young adolescent girls (and boys as well) can be very catty. They talk behind one another's backs and hurt one another unintentionally and intentionally. While the Scriptures don't directly address the adolescent years (wouldn't it be great if the wise King Solomon had written Proverbs for Parenting Adolescents?), one great principle for handling teenage "trash talk" is found in 1 Peter 3:9: "Do not repay evil with evil or insult with insult, but with blessing, because to this you were called so that you may inherit a blessing."

It is hard for adults, and even harder for teens, to respond in this way. When hurt, the natural response is to hurt back; when insulted, to insult back. Your teens' lives are full of opportunities to bless others, but they need your help. Consider the following situation. Eighth-grade Christy sobbed as she said to her mom, "She lied to him about me. I never said that it bugged me when he called. Now he doesn't call and hardly speaks to me. All because of her lie. Oh, I hate her!"

Mom listened to Christy, then tried to identify with her feelings by acknowledging them: "It hurts when a friend lets you down. I know how you feel." Once Christy had calmed down and knew Mom understood, she was more open for suggestions.

Too often parents begin dishing out advice before the teenager has finished explaining the problem, saying things like, "It is wrong to hate!" or "You have got to live your faith." No wonder parents get responses like "You just don't listen. You don't understand at all!"

What is a better way to proceed? The first important step for Christy's mom was simply to listen and try to identify Christy's feelings. She gave her daughter time to cool down. Then together they discussed the principle of giving a blessing for a curse laid out in 1 Peter 3:9. Mom suggested that one way for Christy to give her friend a blessing would be to say something kind to her friend; she then asked Christy what she might do tomorrow at school. Christy wasn't sure she could say something kind, but she agreed to give her friend a smile. A smile is a beginning for all of us.

While peers will always influence your adolescents, the more teens know what they believe and why they believe it, the less susceptible they will be to peer pressure.

Challenge

Make a list of majors that are moral issues that do make a difference in light of eternity. To help you determine whether or not an issue fits the "major" category, use the process below.[7]

1. Write the issue in question.

2. Is this an opinion (a conclusion based on my own feelings or attitudes)?

3. Is this a bias (a conclusion based on a teaching, prejudice, or attitude of a certain group)?

4. Is this a conviction (moral issue that will make a difference in light of eternity—a biblical absolute)?

10

Internalizing Values and Making Wise Decisions

When we asked parents, "What do you want the most for your teen?" some of the answers we received were

- "that we would always have a healthy open relationship with good communication."
- "that my son would own a personal faith in God."
- "that my adolescent would find a spouse with similar values—that family would always be important to her."
- "that my adolescent would know what she believes and would base her life on sound biblical principles."
- "that my child would be a well-adjusted adult and contribute to the betterment of this world."
- "that my teenager would be able to stand alone and make wise choices."

When considering the big issues of life, we didn't hear parents make comments like, "I hope my son will always have a clean room," or "I hope my daughter will never pierce her nose." However, one parent jokingly said, "That my sons don't cuss, drink, smoke, or chew, or go with girls that do."

What do you think of when you look at the big picture? If you had to write in twenty-five words or less what you desire for your adolescent, what would you write?

When we looked at the big picture, we wanted to facilitate our sons becoming all that God desired for them to become—to make a positive impact on others so that our world would be a better place because of their lives. After all, isn't that what we desire for ourselves as well?

A wise friend told us, "If my kids buy into ninety percent of my value system, I will feel I have done a good job of parenting." Our children are not clones. They will go places we will not go and experience things we will not experience. Life goes forward, not backward.

Gibran wrote, "Seek not to make your children like you." While you want to pass on your values and your faith, as parents you need to realize the outworking of the torch you pass on to your children may be somewhat different than you had envisioned. So if your young adults choose different denominations than your own in which to worship God, be thankful they are worshiping God! We see too many parents of young adults who are disappointed in their children's choices and in the fact their children are not carbon copies of themselves. And disappointment translates into strained parent-adult child relationships. So even if you don't see the spiritual maturity you desire in your kids, continue to love and accept them. Do what you can to facilitate their faith, but ultimately, you must trust God with their lives. Be assured that your heavenly Father loves your children even more than you do!

God's care does not relieve you of your part in shaping your kids, of course. By helping them find confidence in themselves and in God, you give them strength that would be difficult to achieve on their own. How can you help foster spiritual growth? Start by addressing things that matter to them. Remember from chapter 1 that one of the seven goals adolescents intuitively seek is "the sense of knowing 'who I am,' of being recognized as a significant person." Of course, the ultimate identity and significance, for all of us, comes from our relationship to our heavenly Father. So how can you help your adolescent realize his own significance? Consider the following true story:

It didn't take long for Bob to let off steam one day when he came home from school. "Boy, did I get burned today! I got into a discussion with Jason about Christianity, and he made me look stupid and ridiculous!"

To help Bob make sense out of his conversation with Jason, Bob's parents set up an appointment for him to talk with a pastor, who was a theologian and a Bible scholar. Bob had a chance to repeat Jason's questions and learn how to respond appropriately.

They offered to host an evening of discussion in their home for their son and his friends.

Together they watched an excellent slide show on the Bible and science and discussed the show afterward.

Several months later, Bob told his mother, "Mom, you won't believe it! One night on the basketball trip we had a fantastic debate about the validity of the Bible—and in the end, Jason even said, 'Gee, I have to admit, your arguments are just as logical as mine!'"

Three years later, Bob as a senior in high school, was brave enough to challenge the head of a university science department in front of two hundred fellow students about the same issue. The professor was impressed enough to look up this student after the lecture and compliment him on his questions.

Who likes to be made fun of or to be considered different? If your adolescents haven't already, they will soon have to face situations like Bob did or to respond to comments such as "Surely you don't actually believe the Bible. Everyone knows it's full of contradictions"; "Christianity is just an outdated religion"; "There are no absolutes—just do what feels good to you." How can you help your children combat such statements? First, it is important to identify with adolescents in their struggles and give them space to question and search for the truth. You can also offer practical help like Bob's parents did.

Whatever the question, you can help your teens explore the subject. Sometimes they are open to your suggestions; other times outside resources are necessary. But you can't do it alone! When children reach the adolescent years, they need other adults who can be role models, and they need friends who share their convictions and standards. If you have a vital youth group in your church, or groups like Young Life and Student Venture at your local schools, count yourself blessed. But if you don't, look around for young adults who you can befriend and who can be a friend to your adolescents.

One warning: We do encourage you to get to know the young adults who influence your children. We have heard both positive and negative stories—and have experienced both. In looking for mentors for your teenagers watch out for the following red flags:

- A young adult of the same sex who has no adult friends
- Someone who monopolizes your teenager's time
- Someone who spends great amounts of time or travel alone with your son or daughter
- Someone who is possessive or jealous of your teen's other friends
- Someone who spends hours on the phone with your son or daughter
- Someone who is overly affectionate with your son or daughter

On the other hand, look for these positive qualities in young adults who are mentoring your teenagers:

- A balanced life with friends his or her own age
- Involvement with other adolescents besides your son or daughter
- A good sense of humor and ability to relate to adolescents
- An active, positive, leadership relationship with a local church or youth organization
- A vital faith in God

One of the best situations we experienced was when we were living in Vienna, Austria. Several wrestlers with Athletes in Action took an interest in our sons and in helping them reach out to their friends. Here's how it started.

We were in a small church with no youth group, so we offered to begin one in our home. Every other Friday after school our teens invited their friends from school to come to our house for what became known as "Friday Pancakes." (Once the group was established we substituted popcorn for pancakes. It wasn't so messy and much simpler!)

The wrestlers took turns leading the pancake parties. Skits, table tennis, videos, and short talks on how your values system and faith can affect your life as a teenager were among the activities. But basically, the group was about having fun and providing a positive environment for our teenagers. The group grew, and we achieved one of our goals of providing a positive peer group for our sons as well as great role models. Years later, we still stay in touch with those wrestlers who now have teenagers of their own!

Let us add, just in case you think relating to adolescents was easy for us, that when we first entered this stage of family life, we were very ill at ease with this age-group. But this was a major in our family so we worked hard to relate to our adolescents and to their friends. Trust us, this is a learned skill!

Do what you can to get your children in a good homogenous peer group. Cultivate their friends and have an "open home" policy. Spend the money on extra gas and give rides to soccer, scouts, and youth groups. Dr. Bruce Narramore reminds us that "parents who know and like their adolescent's friends and are comfortable having them around are much less likely to have problems with negative peer influence."[1]

From Director to Spectator

You can do all you can do, but it is only God who can motivate your teens from within. Internalizing their faith is hard, both for them and for you as you stand by and watch them doubt and question. One parent in a parenting support group expressed her fear this way:

"If I had grown up in a Christian home, perhaps it would be easier to know what is 'normal' for my daughter to go through in internalizing her faith. Both my husband and I became Christians as adults. It's so scary when we see her questioning, searching, doubting, and making statements like, 'I'm not interested in all this religious stuff' or 'I want to run my own life, thank you!'

"It's like she is having an internal war, struggling with the desire to be popular and accepted with her peers. She's walking a tightrope, balancing precariously between commitment to God and commitment to the lifestyle of her peers. At times she seems even hostile and indifferent.

"A friend in her twenties tells me that this is all normal. And I think, 'Oh good—it's normal' but my stomach doesn't understand, and it feels like a huge knot that tightens each time my daughter verbalizes a statement of doubt. I remember the chill I felt when I first realized that she could choose not to put her faith in God and to turn away from all she had been taught. I guess it comes down to simply trusting God for what you can't see. I have to do that in other areas of her life, but somehow it is hardest in the spiritual area."

Making It Their Own

Are you willing to influence your adolescents by your example, by praying for them, and by allowing them the freedom to internalize their faith, to go from outward standards to inner convictions that are their own?

Teens are not free to choose God's way as their own until that choice is presented to them. A belief must be chosen freely from a variety of alternatives. What if your teens leave home with the habit of conforming to your standards? They enter a new world, no longer surrounded by your influence, without convictions of their own. This scenario is played out each fall on college campuses across the country. Older teens experience much confusion (and parents much heartache) as they try to sift through all kinds of new philosophies. How much better it is to encourage your adolescents to begin forming his or her own con-victions while still at home. Several parents give the following tips on how to do this.

Encourage Questions

Let your adolescents know it's okay to ask questions—that you will not overreact, but will help them find answers. One teenager admitted to our parenting group:

"I asked some questions that really surprised my parents. I was the resident cynic in our house. But my parents always encouraged me to question and helped me find answers if they didn't know them. I learned that Christianity is rational and log-ical; it is not the blind faith some say it is."

Remember your teens must have answers. Kids face hot issues in high school like abortion, premarital sex, drugs, alcohol, and so on. They need you to encourage them to decide what they believe.

When well-known theologian Francis Schaeffer's daughter asked her father a number of questions like, "How do I know God exists?" he responded:

"Susan, those are good questions. I'm glad you asked them."

She writes about this experience: "What a relief. That dizzy, lonely feeling left me. It was okay to ask questions! It was impor-tant for me to find out for myself if what I believed was true.

"As we talked that night, I discovered that my dad had asked these same questions about God in his own search for answers. Dad opened the door for me into a new adventure. He said that I didn't have to go through life with a blindfold on my mind to believe in God, merely clinging to hopes and feelings. Neither did I have to throw my beliefs out the window.

"If something is true, he explained, you can look at it hard, and think about it, and compare it with other beliefs, and it will stand. It will be reliable. I decided to do just that."[2]

Provide Good Books and Tapes

Young adolescents are more open to your suggestions, so take advantage of these years to give your children good books and tapes. Here are some of the resources parents in PEP Groups have found helpful:

- *Preparing for Adolescence* by Dr. James Dobson—Available both as a book and as cassette tapes, this is an excellent resource for a parent to listen through with their child. Ideally this should be done before the teenage years.
- *How to Be Your Own Selfish Pig* by Susan Schaeffer Macaulay—A book of apologetics for teens, this resource looks at the "gimme myths" of today's society through the magnifying glass of Christian belief.
- *Campus Life* magazine and website: http://www.christianity.net/campuslife—The online version of *Campus Life* is a relevant cutting-edge Christian magazine for teens. The site features articles from the current issue, complete past issues, message boards, and an offer for a free hard copy of the publication. There are lots of links to other sites (advice, humor, reviews, resources, trends, and stats) that makes this valuable for teens, youth workers, and parents.

Model Your Own Faith

If you sit around and bite your nails, your adolescents aren't going to believe your God is very powerful!

"If you are going to try to teach your children the fundamentals of the Christian faith," one sixteen-year-old girl told a PEP Group, "make sure you teach them convictions, not contradictions. Make sure they see that you live your beliefs. This is the strongest case for your faith.

"For instance, some parents ignore their own mistakes, like the times when they react and get angry at their kids. After all, they're the parents, so they just let it slide. But if my mom is unjust or loses her temper and yells at me she quickly says, 'I'm sorry; I was wrong.'

"How you handle times like this makes your faith valid to your kids. If you also forgive your teenagers when they blow it and love your kids unconditionally, they will know that the faith you are advocating is real and works."

Learning to Make Wise Choices

When dealing with any major issue, your influence as the parent is directly related to the relationship you have with your adolescents. Their learning to make wise choices is dependent upon your majoring on your relationship with them. No longer will they willingly let you be the model or teacher just because you are the parent. So do anything you can do to improve your relationship with your adolescents. We would like to suggest four practical ways you can help your adolescents learn to make wise choices.

Allow Your Teens to Participate in Family Decisions

A number of years ago we had a major decision to make. Our job in Austria was drawing to a close, and we had decided to return to the United States. Our oldest son was nearing college age, and the move to an American school system seemed timely. We had two possible locations—Atlanta, Georgia, or Knoxville, Tennessee, so we decided to bring our boys into this decision-making process. We sat down with each of the boys individually and talked through the pros and cons of each location, making a list as we went. Our boys liked being included in the discussion and their input definitely influenced our final decision. The more family decisions teens can participate in, the more confident they become in their own decision-making ability.

Allow Your Teens to Choose Between Options

Decision making is easier for young adolescents if they are given a choice between two or more options. Our youngest son loved both basketball and skiing, but we knew he couldn't participate in both sports since the seasons overlapped.

"The decision's up to you," we said. "Since both basketball and ski racing have the same season, you must decide which one you want to do this year. You might want to list all the pros and cons of each sport, and then pick the one that seems best."

He decided on ski racing.

Once a decision has been made, we insisted that the boys complete the commitment. For instance, when one of our sons signed up for the soccer league one fall, we encouraged him to stick with it until the season was over, even though he didn't want to. If he wanted to skip the league's spring season, that was all right, but we nudged him to complete the commitment he had made for the fall season.

Part of decision making is encouraging your adolescents to develop their own thinking process. Try answering a question with a question. "Well, what do you think of that?" or "What do you think is the smart thing to do in this situation?" It's easy to give instant answers, but check yourselves before offering advice.

Allow Your Teens to Negotiate

Sometimes teens have no trouble making decisions, but you can't go along with the decisions that they make.

When one of our sons was a senior in high school, he was co-captain of the soccer team with practice every day for several hours after school. He was also working at the local tennis club on the weekends and wanted to add a work night during the week, which would include cleaning up the club after closing and getting home at midnight.

We had our doubts about this. "Let's sit down and talk about it. Get some paper, and let's list the pros and cons."

"Not the pros-and-cons list again!" our son moaned.

"You talk, and we'll write. Now give us all the pros of why you should work on weeknights." We waited patiently.

"Well," he said slowly, "there's money, money, and money."

The pro list completed, we added several cons, such as loss of sleep and effect on studies.

At an impasse, we switched into the negotiation mode, going through the following three steps.

1. We stated the problem clearly: he wanted to work at night during the school week, and we did not want him to.

2. We listed some possible options:
   a. Work only on weekends
   b. Work weekends and one school night
   c. Work weekends and afternoons
   d. Work weekends, two mornings before school, and vacuum the courts sometime during the week (This might involve some night work, but not as late as a complete cleanup.)

3. Choosing a plan of action was the last step we took, and we settled on the last option, subject to the boss's approval, which was given.

Doesn't this take a lot of time? Yes. But we're in the process of helping our teens become competent decision makers. It would be simpler just to say, "Do this" or "Do that," but when would they learn to make their own decisions?

Allow Your Teens to Make Mistakes

The hardest part of teaching teens to make decisions is watching them make mistakes. Consider one parent's story:

"I'll never forget the time Jeffrey took his new Walkman on a ski team trip.

"'Nothing will happen to my Walkman if I take it with me,' he argued. 'It will be so boring without music.'

"'I still don't think it's wise, but the decision is yours to make,' I replied. I had not been in favor of his spending about eighty dollars for it in the first place. That, too, had been his decision.

"Before he turned to go out of the room, I added, 'I want you to do one thing before making the final decision. Take a piece of paper and on one side list all the pros, the reasons you want to take the Walkman. Then on the other side, list all the cons, the reasons you shouldn't take the Walkman. After that, the decision is yours.'

"I expected him to make the right decision once he had weighed the cons against the pros. His paper looked something like this, and from his perspective the decision was obvious."

Pros
1. I want to take it.
2. I'll have music on the bus and won't get bored.
3. If the weather is bad and we can't ski one day, I'll have music.
4. I'll be able to choose what music I want to hear and won't have to listen to trash.
5. It's not heavy and won't be hard to pack.

Cons
1. Can't really think of any, except that there's a slight possibility the Walkman might get lost or stolen.

"'I'm not sure the first item on your pro list, wanting to take the Walkman, is legitimate,' I mentioned. 'It's your wish, not an objective reason.'

"Jeffrey didn't answer, so I asked one more question. 'Are you sure you've considered all the cons? What about the possibility that the Walkman might get wet or be ruined in other ways?'

"'That just adds one more con,' Jeffrey insisted, 'so the pros win. I'm going to take my Walkman.'

"The next day as the bus pulled away from the school, I could see Jeffrey's face, surrounded by the wire headset, in the window.

"Several days later Jeffrey arrived home from the trip minus one Walkman!

"'I hid it under my pillow, I just didn't leave it lying around. Can you believe someone would actually steal it?' he lamented.

"Refraining from answering that question, I said, 'Jeffrey, I'm really sorry it was stolen. I know how hard you worked to save money to buy it.'"

Perhaps you could relate a similar sad story. Jeffrey could not afford to replace the Walkman, but we feel sure he learned from this experience. Losing a Walkman was tough on Jeffrey, but it wasn't a major decision, like buying a computer or choosing a college—for which he used the same decision-making process much more objectively.

If your teens can develop confidence and competence all along the way, then they will learn how to make wise choices when it comes to major issues in life like choosing their values and determining their core beliefs. As scary as it is for parents, these are the steps to adulthood through with each adolescent must go!

Challenge

When dealing with negotiable issues use the following four steps:

1. Adolescents summarize what they want.

2. Each parent summarizes what he or she wants.

3. Together propose alternatives after you have discussed points 1 and 2.

4. Work out a compromise.

PART FOUR

Relax:

Accepting Things You Cannot Change

Adolescent Girls and Boys— Understanding the Difference

In almost every parenting conference, someone asks, "Who are more difficult as teenagers—girls or boys?" Our answer? "Boys, of course!" After all, we had teenage sons. What could possibly be more challenging? Our friends with all girls answer, "Three adolescent girls!" Those with both adolescent girls and adolescent boys say it's mixed, but one thing's for sure—boys and girls are different!

Current research validates this claim. That girls and boys are different is a biological reality. They're not from the same planet—they may not even be from the same universe! Books like *Reviving Ophelia* by Dr. Mary Pipher and articles like "Boys Will Be Boys" in the May 11, 1998, issue of *Newsweek* have put adolescent gender differences on the front burner. Understanding differences, like the varying rough spots along the way to adulthood, will help you better negotiate the adolescent passage. Parents need all the help they can get!

What changes in your teenagers did you encounter as they reached puberty? If you have both a boy and a girl, did their differences at this stage of life surprise you? Some of the changes are predictable and some tend to be a "girl thing" or a "boy thing." Consider some of the gender differences that come with the arrival of your sons and daughters. The *Newsweek* article mentioned above suggests that "child development" research has been replaced by gender development and that girls and boys face different challenges. The article gives a very general breakdown of the gender differences at different ages. For instance, boys are born with larger brains while girls are born with more nerve cells to process information (neither affects intelligence).

Girls tend to adjust better to school and read sooner than boys do. In the early elementary years, boys are more aggressive and excel at gross motor skills. Girls are better at fine motor skills and excel verbally. Then puberty hits. Boys tend to catch up verbally and may pull ahead in math, but their school dropout rate climbs. For girls, puberty may hit them like a hand grenade. It's a very vulnerable time and as many as fifteen percent experience depression. The middle adolescent years bring more challenges. Girls often suffer from eating disorders, while boys may indulge in drugs, alcohol, and aggressive behavior. Girls may also test drinking and smoking, but boys are more likely to binge drink. More girls attempt suicide, but more boys succeed. Both boys and girls face tremendous pressure to conform to their peer group. So whether you have adolescent girls or adolescent boys, you are right to have concerns! Let's look at each gender and consider how in the midst of the adolescent rapids, you can help your teens stay in the boat and not drown.

Help, I'm the Parent of an Adolescent Boy!

Even normal boy behavior may seem problematic in the adolescent years. Their abundance of physical energy and aggressive desire to conquer can get them in all kinds of trouble at school and with parents. Boys have higher levels of testosterone, which feeds their aggressiveness, and lower levels of serotonin, which inhibits aggression and impulsiveness. They are prime candidates for ADD (attention deficit disorder). When our three sons were adolescents we didn't know that term, but we remember their short attention span and endless energy!

What every adolescent boy needs is a strong parental bond, which he may fight against having. With the high rate of divorce, too many boys are growing up without a strong male model. So how can you connect with your teenage son? Any way you can! Researchers report that during the adolescent years the most important protection against developing negative patterns such as smoking, drinking, and even suicide attempts is having a strong parental bond. In chapter 4, we emphasized that children's self-perception is greatly influenced by how they think their parents see them. So spend time building your relationship with your teenage son! It may well be his "life insurance"!

Following are some tips for parents of adolescent boys:

Help channel his energy into constructive activities. Is your son interested in sports? Get involved in coaching, transporting, and supporting your son's interests. We learned how to ski and play tennis. Get involved in what interests your son.

Get to know his friends. The best way to encourage your son to have appropriate relationships is to stay in touch with his friendship circle. We always encouraged our sons to bring their friends to our home. We didn't worry about grass—our yard was the neighborhood soccer practice field—so we wouldn't have to worry about the other kind of grass (the drug kind).

Keep your sense of humor. We know parents of adolescents who used to be so much fun until they had teenagers! A friend who is on the staff of a national youth organization that works predominantly with teenagers told us, "I do great with other people's teenagers, but I tense up when I try to relate to my own adolescent son!" Go buy a joke book. Put cartoons on the refrigerator. Lighten up! When things really get tense, pretend in your mind that your son is in someone else's family. Whatever you're so uptight about may come into perspective.

Express your anger in an appropriate way. Use the anger ladder yourself! Learn to express your negative feelings without attacking your adolescent or defending yourself.

Hug him! Boys also need hugs. They won't admit it, but boys need affection, and they need to be touched. Often you can accomplish this through playing around. Look for ways to make positive physical contact with your teenage son.

Go with the flow. Be flexible. Listen when they want to talk! Look for open communication doors—like times you are in the car or waiting at the dentist. Do all you can to stay connected.

Help, I'm the Parent of an Adolescent Girl!

If your cooperative daughter hasn't hit puberty yet, you may be thinking you really don't need this—but don't skip this section yet! Change is just up ahead.

At a recent parenting conference in Edina, Minnesota, we had very little to say. Instead, the parents who currently had adolescents carried the conversation—we barely got in a word. Their local PEP Group for Parents of Teens attracts those who are getting ready for the adolescent years and often, the leaders told us, parents can't believe that their little darlings are about to hit the rapids of adolescence—not *their* children and especially not their precious little girls!

Recently in our PEP Group we talked about the parent whose thirteen-year-old son wrecked his grandparents' car. One mother immediately reacted: "My daughter would never do that! She is too sweet and obedient. We have taught her to respect the property of others so we won't have problems like that!"

"Just wait," we told her. "Adolescent girls can drive you crazy!"

Then another parent in our conference spoke up. "I know what you are talking about. One day three months before my daughter's thirteenth birthday, she came home a different person. I want to know what happened to my loving and cooperative daughter. She suddenly changed into a different person—a person I don't know and I don't even like! Where is my daughter who was interested in books, sports, people, nature, and life? Now she just sits in front of the mirror totally absorbed with how she looks. Bad hair is a major tragedy and ruins her entire day."

"She hit puberty," we told her. "Everything is changing. And for girls, the changes are more dramatic—her body is changing, mood swings are perpetual, and she communicates with you by arguing."

Besides the predictable physical and emotional changes that occur in puberty, parents must also deal with the negative message today's culture sends to adolescent girls. She is to be pencil thin just when her body begins to round out. If she develops early, she is the object of sexual jokes and comments. Peer pressure adds to the cultural pressure from television, movies, magazines, advertisements, and school. No wonder she is sullen and secretive. Dr. Mary Pipher in her excellent book, *Reviving Ophelia,* writes, "Early adolescence is a time of physical and psychological change, self-absorption, preoccupation with peer approval and identity formation. It's a time when girls focus inward on their own fascinating changes. . . . They blame their parents for their misery, yet they make a point of not telling their parents how they think and feel."[1]

As a parent of an adolescent girl what can you do to counteract the culture? You can start by understanding what your daughter needs. Along with the list of adolescent goals in chapter 1, consider more specific gender needs. Dr. Pipher gives a current overview of the needs of adolescent girls contrasted with her own needs years ago: "While the world has changed a great deal in the last three decades, the developmental needs of teenage girls have changed very little. I needed, and girls today need, loving parents, decent values, useful information, friends, physical safety, freedom to move about independently, respect for their own uniqueness and encouragement to grow into productive adults."[2]

Dr. Pipher's observations give parents of adolescent girls a clue to their daughter's most urgent needs. Let's translate them into some practical tips for relating to your adolescent daughter:

Give unconditional love. Adolescent girls need parents who are mature, basing their love and acceptance not on their daughter's performance, attitude, or mood. Face it, you're the grown-up, so act like it—give unconditional love. One mother told us, "My daughter is having a difficult time growing up, so each morning I give her a clean slate. I erase all the hurts and angry words spoken yesterday, and give her the gift of a fresh start."

Remember that this phase is temporary. Adolescence is time-limited. While some experts now say that adolescence may extend into the early twenties, it *will* come to an end. One day your daughter will be an adult. Let that fact encourage you when your cactus won't let you close.

Concentrate on the relationship. Our central message throughout this book is to keep building an open, honest relationship with your adolescents. At times it will seem as if you are doing all of the work. Teenage girls can be especially caustic, haughty, and rude. Tolerate what you can and do all you can to preserve the relationship. At a critical point it may well be your daughter's lifeline!

Be brave enough to say no. According to Dr. Pipher the best family is the one in which the message children receive from parents is "we love you, but you must do as we say."[3] She points out that adolescents do not deal well with ambiguity. So it's fine to establish limits.

Provide adequate structure. If you haven't already provided a rite of passage into adolescence for your daughter, consider adapting the Teenage Challenge and the Birthday Boxes. Because girls tend to struggle with puberty, she will need the reassurance that she can make it. Providing adequate structure will help her feel safe and in control of her life.

Give a lot of affirmation. Help your daughter to make the most of her best features—whether physical, mental—and look daily for ways to give affirmation. (Review chapter 3.) Encourage her to keep achieving academically, and if she's athletic, to remain active in sports. Encourage her to adopt a healthy lifestyle, which includes a healthy diet. Whenever you can, give her an honest compliment! Whether you believe it or not, if she is like most adolescents, you are her hero.

Summing It Up

Whether you are the parent of adolescent girls or adolescent boys, you can make a difference. You can work with God in helping your children make it through the adolescent passage. Understanding your children's natural bent along with gender differences will help you coach your teens to navigate the risky waters. When discussing adolescents, psychologist Dr. James Dobson was asked why he focuses his comments on parents instead of on adolescents. He responded that when a teenager is about to go over the falls and he is intensely angry at home and is being influenced by a carload of crummy friends, it's the parent who can make the difference. In his newspaper column he cautions parents about being idealists and perfectionists. It's easy to rock the boat. He writes, "Be very careful with him. Pick and choose what is worth fighting for, and settle for something less than perfection on issues that don't really matter." Dr. Dobson's best advice applies equally to adolescent girls and to adolescent boys. He says, "Just get him through it!"[4]

Challenge

If you are the parent of a teenage boy, look again at the parenting tips that apply specifically to young men. Choose one to focus on this week. Here are some suggestions:

- Have one or two of his friends over after school. Provide the snack of his choice.
- Give him a hug every night before bed this week.
- Go out for pizza and talk about his interests and what activities he might like to get involved in.

If you are the parent of a teenage girl, look again at the parenting tips that apply specifically to young women. Choose one to focus on this week. Here are some suggestions:

- Offer to color or highlight her hair this weekend. Go shopping together for just the right color (but let her pick!).
- Look for something positive in your daughter every day this week. First thank God for that quality or action, then praise your daughter, either verbally or with a card left on her pillow.
- Become a member of the "clean slate" club. Before you go to bed, write down the things your daughter did during the

12

Midcourse Correction

During our sons' adolescent years we generally stuck close to home, but on this particular weekend we traveled to another town to conduct our Marriage Alive seminar. While we were away, our three sons stayed with good friends and returned home a few hours before we arrived. As we walked into our home, Claudia immediately smelled cigarette smoke. Following her nose led her to one of our sons. As she gave him a hug and kiss, she confirmed her suspicions. He had been smoking!

Without taking time to gather the facts, she immediately accused him. "You've been smoking! How could you? You've broken our trust."

"No, Mom," he responded to her attack. "I promise I haven't been smoking."

"Then what is that smell?" Claudia probed.

"Some guys were smoking on the bus on the basketball trip last weekend. I am wearing the same clothes, and they must still smell of smoke."

This did not satisfy either of us. After all, how did the smoke from his clothes get into his mouth? And his room smelled of smoke. There were no signs of cigarettes, but when Dave looked out the open window he saw a cigarette butt on the ground outside.

We mentally reconstructed the crime. Our son lit up in his room, then heard us drive in the driveway. He threw the cigarette out the window and then raced into the kitchen. He had forgotten about Claudia's excellent sense of smell. This was not the first time we had talked to him about smoking or lying.

After Claudia's outburst with our son, she realized she had to calm down and get out of the attack mode. This took several hours but later that evening we were ready to talk through the situation. As we began to talk, we purposely avoided the question of "Where did we go wrong?" and instead concentrated on "Where do we go from here?"

Our son still maintained he was innocent, even though his guilt was obvious. Claudia spoke up. "We do believe in miracles, yet we see no way a cigarette could smoke itself in your bedroom and then hop out the window. We would also be dumb to ignore the obvious sign of smoke on your breath."

At this point Dave picked up the ball. "As I see it, we are dealing with two issues here: first, smoking; second, lying. Frankly, we are most concerned with the lying. You've been working hard in this area; don't let a relapse set you back."

After a little more persuasion, our son admitted his mistake and accepted the consequences, the loss of his privileges for a week. We were all ready to move on, but felt we had to renew the trusting relationship, so the next day Claudia wrote this letter:

Dear Son,

Today my thoughts keep coming back to the unbelievable welcome I gave you yesterday. Wish we both could do it over again. So you experimented again with cigarettes—big deal! Growing up, I did the same.

I'm really not concerned that you'll become a smoker. You're analytical and intelligent, and you know cigarettes can be harmful to your health. I trust your judgment in this area. If you choose to smoke as an adult, it's your decision.

What I wish I could change about last night was my initial reaction. I made it very difficult for you to be open and honest with me. If I had waited until I was in control of my own feelings, perhaps you would have chosen honesty instead of deception. Let's work together on this area during the next few weeks.

Our Part: Dad and I will try not to put you on the spot. If you feel like you are being attacked, please say, "Wait, I feel attacked. Let's start this conversation over again."

Your Part: You choose to be open and transparent with us, to tell the truth even if it's incriminating.

Let's build back that trust quickly. I think even twenty-four hours of openness could do it.

Love, Mom

If you've ever tried to release teens, you know it's not without some disappointments and failures like this one. We desperately needed some midcourse correction. Maybe you too from time to time veer off course and need to regroup. Perhaps you can identify with the mom who wrote the following in her journal in a moment of sheer frustration:

"I feel like such a failure. Our family seems to be crumbling apart. Being a parent used to be fun; now it's just one big hassle! I only see the inadequacies in me, my husband, and the children. I'm tired of making decisions (which are usually wrong), of not being respected, of being ignored, of not being appreciated. Tonight I wish I had never had kids.

"I tell my daughter, 'I love you,' and she remains stone-faced. I feel I've tried so hard and that nothing took. Failure is such a terrible feeling. How can I get out of this emotional bondage and get back on a more positive track? I feel hopeless."

Maybe you aren't to this point of desperation, but all parents need midcourse correction from time to time. Let's consider three different situations:

You, like the parent in the letter, have really tried but it just isn't working. Included in this category is the parent who has tried too hard and has pushed his or her teen farther away.

You have a history of bad communication. "It's too late to start trying to build a relationship that appears to be nonexistent," you say. "If only I had worked harder in the elementary years, but somehow the years one to twelve just slipped by."

You have simply given up on yourself and on your teen who senses parental disappointment. You're both surrounded by a fog of hopelessness. What's the use of trying? The relationship is already blown.

Do you identify with any of these situations? If you're the parent of preteens, you may not have reached this state yet. We suggest that you read this chapter so you can make a midcourse correction when you begin to sense some problems. If you're the parent of teens, you may be basically on course and only need some fine-tuning. Or maybe some major adjustments are needed to get back on course.

If the trouble between you and your children is chronic, we suggest that you seek professional help from a counselor or psychiatrist, preferably someone who shares your values. In these pages we are discussing everyday situations where there's time to reinvest and rebuild trust. As long as you have good open communication, rebuilding trust should not be an impossible task.

Good News Ahead

Wherever you are, there is hope for midcourse correction. But it doesn't start with your adolescent. It starts with you. We can't change other people, but we can change ourselves.

The one element that has given us the power to change and apply the principles shared in these pages is our faith in God. Without his involvement in our lives, this book is just another self-help effort without the gas to fuel the good intentions. Consider this: Our heavenly Father is the One who created both us and our children. And he didn't leave us to struggle in the dark. He gives us the principles and the power to implement them in our parent-teen relationships.

Are you allowing God to enlighten your way as you parent your adolescents? Having a relationship with God doesn't guarantee a great relationship with your teens, but it is the best starting place. Stop now and evaluate how you are relating to your child. Do you treat him or her with the same respect and courtesy that you would a good friend? Are you applying the love Paul describes in 1 Corinthians 13? Rachel didn't. Both she and her husband were high achievers in college. They had never considered that their son might be only an average student. In elementary school, Rachel worked with the boy to help him achieve academic success, but in junior high he began to resent his mom's help. Slowly his grades dropped to Bs and Cs. Rachel's own self-esteem was hurt by her son's poor performance and his seeming rejection of her help. Their relationship continued to go downhill. Finally her son decided, *I just can't please my parents, so why try?* His B and C grades became Ds and Fs.

Was Rachel a Christian? Yes. Did she want to be a good parent? Yes. But she didn't realize that her self-worth should come from being a child of God, not from her children and their achievements. She also needed to realize it's all right to be average. As one person said, "God must have a special place in his heart for average people. He made so many of them!"

Don't make the mistake of looking to your children for your own self-worth. Instead, find your security and significance in your relationship with God. The result? You will be free to love your teens with God's unconditional love; and if it's unconditional, it's not dependent on any human response or behavior.

Now it's time to focus on what you can do to improve the relationship with your teenagers. Consider the following two areas that may need attention:

1. Rebuilding trust
2. Learning how to deal more effectively with a resistant teen

Rebuilding Trust

One day Claudia asked one of our sons, "If you could change one thing about me, what would it be?"

He answered without hesitation, "That you would totally trust me!"

Fritz Ridenour, in his book *What Teenagers Wish Their Parents Knew About Kids,* says he tells his parenting classes and seminars one basic thing: "You might as well trust your teenager; you don't have any other reasonable choice. Distrust simply breeds more distrust, but if you keep trusting your teenager, sooner or later the message will get through."[1]

Five Trust-busters

If you do not have a trusting relationship with your kids, now is the time to begin to build trust. Start by thinking about how you lost that natural trust that exists between parent and child. Consider these five possible trust-busters.

Trust-buster 1: A Single Mistake

Adolescents often do something wrong, and the parent responds, "If I can't trust you in this area, how can I trust you in other areas?" Trust is not a one-time gift, however; trust must be freely given time and time again.

After trust has been broken, it's easy to think, "How can I trust my teen again? He deceived me once, so he may do it again."

Unless you are willing to reinvest some trust, your teens have no way to rebuild that trust. You could say something like "This has been a good learning situation, and we feel you're learning the importance of being open and honest with us. That's real progress. Let's continue to work together on this. We believe we can rebuild the trust between us in twenty-four hours." While this may seem like too much pressure or too short of a period of time to restore trust, in our family we found that if we concentrated on restoring trust for even twenty-four hours, we were able to refocus and make progress.

Trust-buster 2: Judging Guilty Without a Fair Trial

Everyone deserves a fair hearing. Do you see your adolescent as innocent until he or she is proven guilty? Unfortunately parents sometimes assume the worst before all the facts are known.

Our friends, Jonas and Candy, were out of town for a week-end, leaving their teenage son home alone. Upon their return, the house was empty, but the kitchen sink was filled with empty beer cans. Jonas told us that his first reaction was to pounce on his son when he returned and demand an explanation as to why he had broken their trust. Instead, he held his tongue and waited for his son to explain the mystery. The truth? The cans had been thrown into the yard and their son was afraid that the neighbors would assume they had thrown a wild party. To avoid the gossip, he had rinsed them out and placed them in the sink until he could dispose of them discreetly.

By assuming the best case scenario—that there must be a logical, innocent explanation—this wise dad avoided breaking the trust with his son. Unfortunately, when our boys were teenagers, at times we were quick to assume the worst before all the facts were known, and at times we convicted them on purely circumstantial evidence.

Trust-buster 3: Lack of Freedom

Sometimes parents communicate to their kids, "Earn my trust, and then I'll trust you." Then they establish ironclad rules that give the teens no leeway.

We ask these parents, "How can your child prove he or she is trustworthy without being given some freedom to make decisions?"

Soon after one of our sons got his license, we let him drive to work at the tennis club. One morning when Dave opened the trunk to get a bag of books he had left there, to his surprise the books were strewn all over the trunk. How could the books be jostled like that? It turned out that our son had been doing figure eights in the empty parking lot of the tennis club. He received a stern lecture about racing around parking lots at night, but we let him continue to drive to work. Why? If we had said, "Earn our trust, and then we'll let you drive again" we would have eliminated his opportunity to be more careful in the future. Real parental trust cannot exist without some adolescent freedom.

Trust-buster 4: Reciting a Litany of Failures

Parents tend to recall a teen's past mistakes and failures whenever their adolescent talks back or argues with them. Sometimes they have really never forgiven the teen for that earlier mistake.

A sixteen-year-old girl told us, "My dad won't let me forget the one night I came in drunk. You'd think he'd realize it was a terrible experience for me. I'd never had anything to drink before, and I got sick and threw up in my date's car. I was horrified.

"I told Dad all about it, but now, whenever I go out, he tells me not to drink and reminds me of that night. Why can't he just give me another chance?"

We can understand the dad's fears for his daughter, but constantly reminding the girl of this failure will not build trust. Why didn't he thank her for telling him the truth? Then they could have talked through the experience together—why it happened and what she might do if she were confronted again with the same temptation.

Trust-buster 5: Parental Evasion of the Problem

Sometimes parents react to a preteen's lying or sneakiness by talking about trust rather than by discussing the individual incident and how to solve it. "How can I trust you when you are continually lying to me?" the parent asks.

Instead, the parent could say, "Look, we want to build our relationship, not tear it down. It would help tremendously if I could count on your being honest with me. Let's try this for a week. I'll try not to attack you, and you try to stick to the truth."

Beginning Again

Obviously the first way to rebuild trust is to determine to avoid these five trust-busters. Replace the negative with the positive by giving the gift of trust to your teens. This seemingly risky and costly investment has been known to pay excellent dividends.

Dr. Norm Wright gives this advice: "Trusting your teen means running the risk of having that trust broken. It might be nice if you could get your adolescent to promise in writing not to betray your trust; you could even get it notarized. But it would only be a piece of paper. As in any love relationship, you have to risk being hurt. You'll be disappointed, just as I've been at times. That's the price of saying, 'I still love you.'"[2]

What if your teens lie again and again or if drug abuse or some other major issue is involved? Surely, you don't just put your head in the sand and blindly trust. At this point you may think your teens have given up their privacy rights by default, and you as a parent must do what you can to supervise and direct your misguided children.

Trust Yourself

You not only need to trust your teens, you need to trust yourself. We tried to be good parents. We majored on family. We weren't always consistent with our boys, but over the years we consistently tried to be. You might have a specific plan, like the Teenage Challenge and Birthday Boxes. Sometimes they work. Other times you have to hope that your common sense will get you through the difficult times.

Trust God

Trust God. We were able to keep going when we hit hard places with our teens because we knew God was totally committed to us and to our sons. How do we know this? Listen to God's promise in Psalm 138:8: "The LORD will perfect that which concerns me" (NKJV).

When you need hope for the future, remember verses like "if we hope for what we do not see, we eagerly wait for it with perseverance" (Rom. 8:25 NKJV) and "the plowman plows . . . in the hope of sharing in the harvest" (1 Cor. 9:10). Look for a concordance that lists all of the verses with the word "hope" in them. When you are feeling blue, read through some of these verses.

Turn Concerns into Prayers

Pray. During the active parenting years we kept a prayer diary for each of our boys. Each year as we set goals for our family, we also made out a prayer list for each son for the coming year. Then we kept that list where it was accessible—like in our Bible or day planner. Some of the items on our list for one son when he was almost thirteen were:

1. His relationship with God would be alive and growing.
   a. He would have confidence that God's way is best.
   b. He would develop a regular devotional time.
   c. He would apply biblical knowledge to daily situations.
   d. He would see answers to his prayers.

2. He would have a high standard of conduct and develop the right convictions.

3. He would work toward academic success.
   a. He would develop a love for reading.
   b. He would give his studies his best effort.
   c. He would work toward good relationships with teachers and other students.

4. He would develop a healthy self-concept.

When we made our concerns our prayers, we found we didn't nag our teens as much. The problems were in God's hands so we didn't have to worry. When a prayer was answered, we wrote the answer across from the request and dated it. This encouraged us on the days we didn't see answers.

Our belief that God loved and cared for our adolescents helped us when we were in the middle of dealing with resistance.

Dealing with a Resistant Teen

"It's not that my daughter is not pliable, she's completely brittle," one parent commented to us. "There's no flexibility at all. When we disagree, there's always resistance."

How can you deal with resistant teens? If we could answer that question, we would retire and move to Bermuda! However, we can say that the younger the resistant adolescents are, the easier it is to improve the relationship.

While strong-willed adolescents are more likely to be resistant, a strong will can be a positive characteristic. When our sons toyed with rebelling, we often reminded ourselves to look at the leaders of our world. It was their strength of will that made them such great leaders.

Claudia recently told one of our sons, "I'm glad you didn't become a rebellious teen." Then she asked him, "What kept you from it?"

"I just decided not to," he answered bluntly.

Later, she asked him again. "You said you were tempted to be rebellious, but you chose not to be. What advice would you give to teens who feel rebellious?"

He thought for a while, then he answered, "Well, I would tell them, 'You might get what you want for a while, but in the end, no one will win.' It's as if you're standing on the edge of a cliff. Why don't you jump off? Because you know what the end results would be."

Our son had weighed the benefits against the final consequences. When he put staying out all night or some other adventure on one side of the scale and his relationship with his parents on the other, the relationship tipped the scales.

Here are some tips from some parents who learned to cope with their resistant teens:

Give Teens as Much Freedom as Possible

Tightening the noose only causes resistant teens to struggle against you even more. Say yes whenever possible. Always ask yourself, "Is this a moral issue?"

Your strong-willed teens will respect you much more if you are consistent. Discuss the issue, let your teens express feelings freely, and if you make a mistake, admit it. But do not be talked into a verdict reversal just to get your teens off your back. If you have to say no, make sure your no remains a no.

One summer one of our sons worked as a counselor at a Boy Scout camp in Germany. During that time we lived in Vienna, Austria, and had planned our family vacation so we could pick up our son at the end of the camping season, which was ten days before his school began.

One night he called us from the camp and excitedly told us about an Air Force sergeant he had met. Then he said, "Sergeant Brooks has invited me to spend a whole week with him at Ramstein Air Force Base. Isn't that great? You won't have to pick me up. I can take a train back to Vienna.

"While he works, I can watch videos, and visit the PX, where I can buy Pop Tarts and Dr. Peppers," he exclaimed. (American goodies we could not buy in Austria!)

We had learned not to give immediate answers to major questions, so Dave told him we would call him back. Many factors led to our final decision to say no: We didn't know Sergeant Brooks; we had planned our vacation around picking him up and saving the price of a train ticket; and we felt he needed the few days of rest before school started.

Our phone discussions were heated after we told him our decision, but in the end he was willing to go along with us. Did he think we made a mistake? Yes! (Even now, years later, he sincerely believes we were wrong. And we still believe we were right.) Was it hard to work through this with our son who was so strong-willed? Yes. Plus we had to work it out through long-distance phone calls! Resistant teens tend to resist accepting their parents' decisions. But if you give as much as you can, the few big nos are more likely to be accepted. Again, let us add that this approach may work with young teens whose parents still have good leverage, but not with older teens.

Respect Your Teen's Privacy

Merton Strommen reminds us: "Respect for the privacy of adolescents, an important aspect of nurturance, indicates parents' belief in their children's right to have a life space of their own. More than that, it is an important ingredient in building trust. Parents who listen to phone conversations or open and read letters are violating the adolescent's desire not to reveal every aspect of himself or herself to others. Throwing out clothes, magazines, or records belonging to the adolescent, or going through desk and dresser drawers, are actions that often result in alienation instead of togetherness."[3] Snooping erodes relationships and breeds distrust. Trust God to reveal to you the problems you need to know.

Resist the Urge to Dote

The more you can relate on an adult-to-adult level with your resistant teens, the better. Three classic books that have helped many parents in our PEP Groups for Parents of Teens live with resistant teenagers are *Parents in Pain* by John White, *How to Really Love Your Teenager* by Ross Campbell, and *The Wounded Parent* by Guy Greenfield. Current books we recommend are: *Parenting With Love and Logic* by Foster Cline and Jim Fay, *Parenting Adolescents* by Kevin Huggins, *Parenting Teens* by Bruce Narramore and Vern Lewis, *Parenting Today's Adolescents* by Dennis and Barbara Rainey, and *Bound by Honor* by Gary and Greg Smalley.

Summing Up

Fritz Ridenour sums up midcourse correction when he says, "After parenting three kids of my own, and talking to a lot of them I didn't parent, I am convinced that the relationship between parent and child is primary. Whatever happens between you and your teenager is commentary on the kinds of attitudes you are bringing to that relationship."[4]

A change in your relationship with your adolescent can start today. Start by giving your child a gift of trust.

Challenge

What can you do this week to broaden your trust of your teens? Here are some suggestions to get you started:

- Start by confessing to God any fears that you have regarding your children. Acknowledge that God is bigger than your fears and loves your children even more than you do.
- Ask God to help you let go of your teens' past mistakes. Determine that you will not bring them up again.
- Give your teen a bit more freedom in an area that may be minor (in the grand scheme of things) but has perhaps been a pet peeve for you (e.g., wardrobe, hairstyle, pierced ears—or other body part!).
- Give your teens added privacy. What about a phone extension in their rooms?
- Consider some of the major issues that your teens have been "hammering" you on. Ask God to give you the strength to stand your ground and be consistent. If you need to revise an earlier decision, ask him for the courage to face your teen with it.

CHAPTER
13

Relax! Who Me?

The week that our oldest son graduated from high school was unbelievably hectic. Still we surveyed our first graduate with pride, for he was fast becoming an adult.

One evening during graduation week Jarrett's friend Andy was staying overnight, and at ten o'clock, Jarrett announced, "Mom, Andy and I need to run over to Andy's house to pick up something. I'll call you from there."

"Don't you dare," Claudia replied. "I'm exhausted. I'm going to bed."

Claudia is a light sleeper and never developed the ability to sleep soundly when an Arp teen was still on the loose. She woke up at 2:00 A.M. and discovered that Jarrett and Andy were still not home.

What do you do when you wake up and your teen is not home? Do you call the hospital? The police? Only a parent who has experienced it knows that helpless feeling when there is really nothing you can do. Although she felt that Jarrett was probably all right, she still had a gnawing feeling in the pit of her stomach as slowly the minutes turned into half an hour and finally an hour. At three o'clock she heard the car turn into the driveway. How did she feel? Relieved. Tired. Angry. Mostly, though, thankful that Jarrett and Andy were safe.

"Jarrett," Claudia began, "I was afraid you and Andy had been in an accident. Do you know what time it is? Where have you been, and why are you dressed like that?"

"Gee, Mom," our smooth-talking son replied, "thanks for worrying about us."

Worrying is not our favorite activity, but it's nice to be appreciated. Just where had these two dignified high school graduates been, dressed in army fatigues with camouflaged faces? They had been writing a toilet-paper greeting to a girlfriend in her backyard!

Are you awakening in the night, wondering where your teen is? Are you worrying about your teen's grades, latest fad, choice of music, friends, or college selection? Are you fearful when you hear a siren? Anxiety tends to appear in parents who feel responsible for events that are often out of their control.

For years you spend your time and energy training your children. Now that they are teens they must begin to make their own decisions. There are still times for advising, but there are also times for letting go. It's hard to watch them squirm under the pressure of peers or too many commitments, to see them crushed by unthinking friends and carried away on a sea of emotions. Relax in the middle of all this? How can parents relax when they feel responsible for things they can't control?

Flying the Bumps

Perhaps you, like our friend Tonya, are not always relaxed on airplane trips, especially the bumpy ones! Tonya told us, "I work so hard helping the pilot when I fly, I never relax. Besides it's hard for me to pray on my knees with my seat belt fastened!"

Once when she was flying in bad weather, with each bump, she thought of a new threat. Maybe we are getting into a hurricane. Maybe we'll hit a wind shear!

Then the captain came on the loudspeaker and said, "For the next hour or two it will be a little bumpy, since we are flying just on top of the clouds. After about an hour, it should be a smooth flight." Tonya began to relax now that she knew to expect a few bumps. "How great to know," she told us, "I was traveling on top of the bumps!"

The teenage years are like that rough flight. Realizing you're on top of the bumps will help you relax, and if you can relax during these years, you can look forward to smooth flying in years to come. However, there are two personality types who seem to have trouble relaxing. Do you recognize yourself as one of these?

The Interference Runner

Do you ever feel you should be a blocker for the local high school football team because you spend so much time running interference between your teen and his dad? Margaret had worked at trying to release her daughter, Jill. She felt she was doing well, especially on this lovely Saturday morning. Jill and her younger brother had each spent the night at a friend's house, and Margaret was relaxing and enjoying a second cup of coffee with her husband when the phone rang. Jill was getting her hair cut by herself this morning, and her mother thought Jill was calling to be picked up.

"Oh, Mom, I'm ruined!" Jill sobbed. "He cut the top too short and left the back too long! Dad will shoot me. My friends will laugh at me!"

"We'll see if it can be fixed," Margaret said to soothe her daughter. "I'll come for you immediately." As she hung up the phone, Margaret also wondered what Jill's dad would say. He didn't like anything extreme, especially odd hairstyles.

When they entered the house, Margaret quickly joined Jill in the bathroom to attempt to repair the damage with water, a blow dryer, and a curling iron. Dad's reaction was, "Why didn't you go with her to make sure the haircut was done correctly?"

Margaret knew he wasn't ready for an explanation of the four Rs and the principle of releasing teens. She felt as if it was the fourth quarter and she was losing!

Some parents are afraid to tell their spouses when a teen has lied or gotten into trouble, because they are afraid the other parent will become angry and blow their relationships with their child. Others must run interference in other areas, between brothers and sisters or grandparents and grandchildren or teens and teachers, and this certainly interferes with relaxation.

The Life Shaper

Often parents take each event too seriously. Many events and decisions are out of their control, so they become frustrated. Others, in their desire to protect their children, sometimes give them too much help.

The year our oldest son was applying to colleges, Claudia succumbed to the life-shaping urge. Fortunately, a good friend reminded her that she was trying to give too much help, so she backed away and allowed our son to be responsible for the deadlines. Although not every application was sent, no deadline was missed for the schools he was really interested in. It's hard to stand by when your teen procrastinates with a reading assignment or misses cheerleading practice. You could remind him about these things, but from past experience you know a friendly reminder can be counterproductive.

One teen told his dad, "You don't have to tell me the obvious like, 'Isn't it wonderful that you have a snow day so you can get caught up on your schoolwork.'"

Character is often built through failure. Allow your teens to make some mistakes while they are still living at home—even though it is scary to think about all the mistakes they can make. How can you relax? Here are four ways other parents have managed to relax during these trying years.

Relaxation Aid 1: Get a Life! Develop an Interest Just for You

Often your teens zaps your emotional energy, and you seem to have less time for yourself. It's good to develop some activities of your own. You might join a volunteer organization whose goals coincide with your own interests. For instance, if you like to help people who are sick, you might want to volunteer a couple of hours a week at the local health clinic. You might join or organize a PEP Group for Parents of Teens.

Physical activity can help you overcome the emotional stress of dealing with adolescents. You can vent your anger and process your disappointments when you hit the tennis ball, do aerobics, jog, or swim. Find some physical outlet.

Relaxation Aid 2: Build the Relationship with Your Spouse

Studies show that two of the most difficult times in a marriage are when children are toddlers and again when they are teens. One husband commented, "We seem to disagree more now about the children than ever before." Another parent added, "It seems our whole relationship is centered around our teenagers, discussing their problems and trying to come up with solutions or discussing our own hurt feelings. It's as if we're not people anymore, just parents of teens. This must stop!"

What can you do to build your relationship with your spouse? We suggest that you begin to date again. Take time each week to be alone and to grow together in your marriage. You may be wondering, *When would we ever find time with all our teens' activities?*

Why not have breakfast or lunch together each week? One couple we know has a standing date each Monday evening while their daughter is at Girl Scouts. You might begin by having some of the dates we suggest in our books *10 Great Dates* and *52 Dates for You and Your Mate*. Remember the precaution: Discussing your teen is an absolute no-no on these dates.

Also, consider a weekend away alone with your mate to concentrate on your marriage, and forget the children for a few days. We try to do this several times a year. In a few short years, your teens will be gone, but life and your marriage will go on. Or you may want to read our book *The Second Half of Marriage*, which lets you know there is life after the kids leave home. Start building today for your future as well as your teens'.

Relaxation Aid 3: Get Enough Sleep and Rest

Late nights are as much a part of caring for a teenager as they are caring for a baby. Weekends, which used to be reserved for family fun, are now work times for parents. One wise mom in a PEP

SAFE ECONOMICAL
MOVING SERVICE

Use Arps' Moving Service
10 cents an item. We aim to please.

The boys got the point, and sometimes even paid their moving bills.

Another time one of our sons received an invitation to a Room Cleaning Party. And from time to time all our kids got a Grump Coupon!

GRUMP COUPON

Good for Two Hours as a Grump
To redeem, simply present
coupon to Mom or Dad.

Look for the humor in each heavy or irritating situation. Once one of the boys and Claudia made the same mistake. She left her garden shoes and he left his soccer cleats just outside the back door. The next morning one of each was missing. We still laugh and look for the neighborhood dog who wears one soccer cleat and one garden shoe. Remember, laughter and relaxing go together.

The Road Has a Destination

We remember having thoughts like, *Isn't it great? Our guys seem to be on the right track. Soon it'll be smooth sailing. Before we realize it, the last one will be gone from the nest and the honeymoon will begin again.*

Our daydreams were interrupted by a dear friend who was well into the empty nest. She reminded us that grown children

Group told how each Monday morning after getting her teens off to school, she would crawl back in bed and sleep until noon.

Since this routine is not practical if you have a job outside of the home, perhaps you could keep Monday nights free so you can go to bed early. Try to plan a light schedule for Fridays in anticipation of a busy weekend.

Relaxation Aid 4: Develop a Sense of Humor

If joking comes naturally in your home, you're fortunate. Some families are natural cutups while others have to work hard to keep the atmosphere light. We still place cartoons and jokes on the refrigerator door, a carryover from the teenage years. Cartoons help us to look for the humor in each situation, like the famous case of "The Twinkle-Toes Scuffs."

You know how discouraging it is to clean and wax the kitchen floor, and then, only a few hours later, find new black scuff marks. This continually happened at our house so finally, in desperation, Claudia put a notice on the refrigerator door:

WANTED:
NOTORIOUS TWINKLE-TOES

$1.00 reward
to anyone giving information leading
to the identification of
Twinkle-Toes, the criminal who
leaves black marks on the
kitchen floor.

The response? Light laughter from our boys and fewer scuff marks.

To solve the problem of the schoolbooks, jackets, and soccer cleats that were cluttering the small hall between our back door and the kitchen, we created Arps' Moving Service. We began with a media campaign (notices on the refrigerator door):

return with spouses and children and that the family grows. There are more relationships to nurture and more opportunities to stay humble.

As you continue down the road of life, stop to pick the flowers along the way. Enjoy each unique and developing adolescent. Embrace the moments of love. Stop fearing the future or pulling up the plant to examine the roots. Instead enjoy the good times and look toward a wonderful future, which will not be perfect but will be shared with adult children who love and respect their parents.

It's the relationship that counts. Today. Tomorrow. And forever.

Challenge

1. Think of areas that you feel responsible for but cannot control. Commit these areas to God each night before you go to sleep.

2. What interests do you have outside the home? If none, list something to pursue.

3. What can you do this week to build your relationship with your mate?

4. List several ideas that might add humor to your relationship with your teen.

PART FIVE

Discussion Guide

Before You Begin*

Welcome to the *Suddenly They're 13!* discussion guide. Over the coming weeks, you will be leading a parenting discussion group using this book. Together, you will build a loving, caring community. You'll tell your own stories to each other; you'll talk about your hopes, fears, and dreams as you look forward to your children actually reaching adulthood. You'll laugh together—and at times you may even cry—but in the process, you'll encourage each other. You will strive for a balanced, biblical view of parenting and relating to your young adolescents. And most of all, you'll discover that nobody has it all together. It's okay to be an "in process" parent.

As the discussion leader, you have the potential to impart great hope and encouragement to other parents. The best tip for being an effective facilitator is to be real. This is not a job for a super-parent! All parents in your group need to feel accepted and comfortable, so your goal should be to communicate love, acceptance, and interest to each participant. After the discussion, they should leave encouraged, knowing that they are not alone in this huge job of parenting adolescents.

Although this discussion guide can be used by individuals or couples, it is ideally suited for a small group study and has already been used over the years by thousands of parents. It can, however, be approached in a variety of ways. You may want to combine several chapters to complete the study in six to eight weeks, or you may choose to meet every other week, or use as a thirteen-week Sunday school curriculum. This study can also be used with the PEP Groups for Parents of Teens video curriculum. (For information about the accompanying video curriculum, see the Marriage Alive Resource information page in the back of this book.)

Before you begin, consider the following tips for facilitating your group:

Encourage group participation. Every member is important, and as the discussion leader you are also part of the group. Group-centered leadership trusts the group's capacity to solve its own problems and knows that the group as a whole is smarter than any one member—including the leader.

*All notes to the leader are in boxes.

Keep the group to a manageable number. A group of eight to ten people works well. A group that is too large cannot function effectively unless it breaks down into smaller units for discussion purposes.

Prepare for each session. Pray for each participant. Also, the questions come out of the context of the chapters in this book, so you need to be familiar with the content, or the discussion is likely to be stilted.

Be flexible. Some groups will want to start the discussion by sharing their own experiences since the last session. Groups are different and the dynamics will change from time to time, so keep a balance between structure and spontaneity. Every question does not have to be used. Follow the leading of the Holy Spirit and you will be fine.

Develop accountability by establishing guidelines. You may want to use a simple contract that each parent signs, which would include the following:

Sample Contract

As a member of this group, I agree to:

Keep confidentiality. (This insures mutual respect and will help parents relax and trust the group.)

Listen to others with empathy and with an open mind.

Avoid giving advice unless I am asked for it; never criticize or condemn.

Take responsibility for my own situation only, not anyone else's.

If possible, read the assigned chapter and complete the exercise before the discussion.

Ready, Set, Go

The difference between reading a book and having it affect your life is involvement. Being a part of a *Suddenly They're 13* discussion group will help you make needed changes and make progress in your relationship with your own adolescents. As you give and receive support and encouragement, you will keep a positive perspective and focus. The emphasis of this study is on creating your own game plan for releasing your children into adulthood and building a better relationship with your adolescent as you go through the process. So get ready; this study will be a time of positive reinforcement!

Introduction:
The Four Rs for Successfully
Parenting Adolescents

Goals

- To define expectations and build a sense of community
- To introduce the four Rs of building relationships with adolescents

Welcome parents. Let parents introduce themselves, give the ages of their children, and share their expectations for the group. For a fun icebreaker, ask parents to describe themselves as they were at age thirteen.

Getting Started

As a parent of an adolescent, it's easy to feel inadequate, frustrated, and overwhelmed. Here's an opportunity to join other parents for a time of mutual encouragement as you share practical tips for preparing for and getting through the adolescent years. You will discover the secrets of communicating with your own "cactus."

You will learn the four "Rs" of building great relationships with adolescents:

Regroup: Evaluate yourself, your adolescent, and your relationship.

Release: Design your own rite of passage and "de-parenting" plan to graduate your child into adulthood.

Relate: Learn how to get off the lecture circuit and major on the majors.

Relax: Get a life—there is light at the end of the tunnel.

> Present guidelines and, if appropriate, have parents sign the group contract.

Group Discussion

1. For each of your teenagers, discuss the following:
What makes your adolescent so unique?

Reflect on your child's birth.

What was your child like at age two?

What was your child like at age ten?

How would you describe your adolescent right now?

Where are you right now in your relationship with your adolescent?

Briefly describe your current relationship with your adolescent.

Briefly describe what you would like your relationship with your adolescent to be.

2. What areas in your relationship need improvement?

3. What goals do you have for your relationship with your adolescent?

> Bring the discussion to a close and summarize.
> Give assignment for next session: read chapter 1 and complete this week's challenge.

1

Will the Well-Rounded Teenager Please Stand Up?

Goals

- To better understand your teenagers' strengths and weaknesses and recognize each teen's unique personality and goals
- To understand your own basic personality temperament and parenting style

Getting Started

Studying your adolescents' personalities and recognizing general adolescent goals encourages you to concentrate on their strengths and to help them strengthen the weaker areas. Being as alert to your own weaknesses as you are to your children's helps you to understand how your own temperament affects your relationship with your teens.

Group Discussion

1. Briefly review the four personality types the book discusses:

Sally Sparkle
Take-charge Thomas
Laid-back Larry
Roller-coaster Renee

2. What other systems of personality analysis are you familiar with? (The Myers-Briggs Type Indicator, developed by Isabel Briggs, classifies people according to four polarities—introvert or extrovert, sensing or intuitive, thinking or feeling, judgment

or perception. D-I-S-C, a fourfold profile developed by Personal Dynamics Institute, includes the dominant, influencing, steady, and compliant. Donna Partow, in her book *A Women's Guide to the Temperaments,* uses the categories of Popular Teen, Perfect Teen, Powerful Teen, and Peaceful Teen.)

3. What is the value of seeing others in terms of a personality profile?

4. What are the dangers?

5. Which parenting style do you most identify with?

6. What kind of parenting do each of the personality types need? For instance, what parent style will best motivate a Laid-back Larry?

7. What would you say are your adolescents' goals? How would they compare with the list from the Strommens? Rate your adolescents on a scale of one to ten, one being this need is not being met; ten being this need is definitely being met!

- Achievement
- Friends
- Feelings
- Identity
- Responsibility
- Maturity
- Sexuality

8. How can you help your adolescents achieve these goals in an appropriate way?

> Summarize discussion.
> Give the assignment for next session: read chapter 2 and do this week's challenge.

2

No Strings Attached

Goals

- To deal with past inappropriate responses toward your teens and ask for forgiveness
- To accept your adolescents with no strings attached

Getting Started

Parents are the adults and must take the lead in turning the negative to positive. That often involves apologizing when you blow it! Then you are to accept your children as God accepts you—unconditionally. As you accept your children for who they are, you create a climate where they can flourish. Then your home can be a secure haven for your adolescents as you seek to gradually release them into adulthood.

Group Discussion

1. What might an appropriate response be in a similar situation in the future?

Have a volunteer read Matthew 7:3–5. Talk about the concept of "Plank Removal." Ask for participants brave enough to share specific situations of reacting to their adolescents. After they share, ask them some growing questions.

2. How do you see your own faults manifested in your adolescents? Are these the ones that really irritate you?

3. What challenges you the most about your adolescents—the ways you are alike, or the ways you are different?

4. How will accepting some of your teens' differences reduce conflict?

5. How can we forgive ourselves (see 1 John 1:9)?

6. How can we forgive our children?

7. Why is it so hard to apologize to adolescents?

8. How can we communicate to our adolescents that we accept them with no strings attached?

Summarize discussion.

Give assignment for the next session: read chapter 3 and do this week's challenge.

3

Bird Legs, Braces, and Zits

Goals

- To learn how to encourage and build up your adolescents
- To resist the urge to push children based on parental needs

Getting Started

Early adolescence is one of the most fragile times of a person's life. You need to be sensitive to this age range, and to develop good habits of genuine encouragement. A large part of your teens' self-concept comes from how they think you view them.

Group Discussion

1. What kinds of insecurities did you experience as a young adolescent?

2. Name two things that helped you feel good about yourself as a teen.

3. Discuss the three pitfalls listed on pages 48–50:

We want our children to excel in our choices.
We want our children to excel in everything.
We push our children too soon.

4. What is your definition of "praise"?

5. What are some ways you can affirm your adolescents? What are some ways you can give nonverbal affirmation?

6. Read Philippians 4:8 and quickly list four of your children's positive attributes.

7. What success have you experienced so far as a member of this discussion group?

> Summarize discussion. Give the assignment for next session: read chapter 4 and do this week's challenge.

The Launching Pad

Goals

- To adjust to the new identity of your children as teenagers
- To develop a rite of passage for your preteens into the teenage years
- To learn how to let go

Getting Started

Many of life's major life transitions or "passages" are marked by a celebration or ceremony—such as weddings, birthdays, graduations, and so on. But what about the passage from childhood to adulthood? Most ancient societies, and many primitive ones today, have some celebration, often including a test of endurance called a rite of passage. Think for instance of the Jewish bar mitzvah or bat mitzvah.

You can help your preteens gain that much-needed sense of achievement by giving them a Teenage Challenge to help them prepare for the teenage years. This rite of passage helps to meet the adolescents' need for achievement. It's a way to say, "We now recognize you as a young adult. You are no longer a child." Why not plan your own "rite of passage" for your child?

Group Discussion

1. What is the advantage for parents of positively recognizing the young person's transition to young adulthood?

2. What are the benefits of having the young person meet a series of goals or achievements?

3. Discuss the steps to designing a Teenage Challenge (see page 65–66).

4. What are some possible challenges under the four areas:

Physical
Mental
Spiritual
Practical

5. How can you make the challenge measurable?

6. How can you best arrive at a consensus between your ideas and your teens' ideas?

7. How can you make sure this Teenage Challenge is really their challenge—not yours?

8. What if your adolescent is already thirteen? How could this rite of passage be adapted (driving challenge, high school challenge, sixteenth birthday challenge, dating challenge)?

> Summarize discussion. Give the assignment for next discussion group: read chapter 5 and do this week's challenge.

5

The Birthday Box

Goals

- To learn how to release
- To develop a controlled plan of losing control so that by the time adolescents leave home, they will be able to function as adults and make wise decisions

Getting Started

The goal of parenthood is to work oneself out of a job. It's an old adage, but a true one. Your objective is to bring your teens gradually to complete independence, which involves adjustment for both parents and teens. One person said, "My goal is to raise my children to be independent of me and dependent on God." To communicate your goal of independence, work out your own plan of release.

Group Discussion

1. How does the "Birthday Box" concept relate to the Teenage Challenge you talked about last session?

2. In what areas do you need to have a plan of release? (What do your children need to know when they leave home?)

3. At present are you releasing too much or not enough freedom to your teens?

4. At present are you giving your teens too much or not enough responsibility?

5. Are you presently giving an appropriate balance of freedoms and responsibilities?

6. How does this balance relate to the concept of natural consequences?

7. What will you do if your adolescents do not handle their boxes well?

8. How will you gauge success or growth (translated into new responsibilities and privileges for your adolescents), using the four factors listed below?

- Attitude
- Spiritual growth
- Academics
- Management of box

9. In your experience, what are the areas in which it is hardest to release?

10. How will releasing your teenagers into adulthood affect your own life?

Summarize discussion and give assignment for the next session: read chapter 6 and do this week's challenge.

6

Getting Off the Lecture Circuit

Goals

- To better listen and relate to your teens
- To identify and correct common listening errors, and to learn the skills of active, empathic listening

Getting Started

To listen is to love. Yet truly listening to someone, especially an adolescent, is hard to do. To avoid the common listening pitfalls of interrupting, lecturing, acting shocked, judging, and so on, learn to listen with the heart. Also, teenagers need emotional and physical space to help them deal with the change going on in their lives. To encourage communication, watch for open gates and develop common interests.

Group Discussion

> Ask a volunteer to read James 1:19 and discuss the principles in this passage.

1. How can you listen to your teens and avoid overreacting?
2. Make a list of listening mistakes such as half listening, saying, "Yes, but . . ." and interrupting to tell your adolescents what they should have done. The list might include things like

reacting with shock
lecturing, condemning, or scolding

giving advice—trying to solve the adolescents' problem
interrupting with irrelevant information

Optional activity: Let parents role-play.

3. Think about how you would react in the following situations:

One of your adolescents tells you about a fight at school.

One of your adolescents tells you she doubts the Bible.

One of your adolescents brings home a report card with an F.

One of your adolescents comes down to breakfast dressed inappropriately for school.

One of your adolescents uses inappropriate language.

4. What would you identify as your most common listening error?
5. What constitutes good listening?
6. What are some positive principles of good listening?

Guide 1: Listen in ways that encourage expression of feelings

Guide 2: Listen to discern your adolescents' perspective (use feedback responses to show that you are trying to understand)

7. What communication activities do you have in common with your adolescents?
8. Where are the communication centers in your home?
9. How can you give physical and emotional space to your adolescents?

Summarize discussion and give assignment for the next session: read chapter 7 and do this week's challenge.

When the Bridge Is Out

Goals

- To learn positive ways to handle parent-teen conflicts
- To learn how to process and deal with anger
- To learn how to cut down on communication failures

Getting Started

Sometimes the adolescents burn the bridge that connects you to them. Other times you have to say no and that burns the communication bridge. How can you learn to say no and to express anger in an appropriate way? Adolescents have a lot of anger, and they need to be able to process it. Using the anger ladder, you can teach them how to deal with their anger. You'll never win the popularity contest with your teens, but you can maintain a healthy relationship with them—even when you have to work through conflict and communication failures. Home should be where you prepare for the battle, not fight it!

> Refer parents to the anger ladder on page 105.

Group Discussion

1. Why do parents hesitate to say no to their adolescents?

2. Discuss using "I-messages" instead of "you-messages" first developed by Dr. Thomas Gordon in his book *Parent Effectiveness Training*.[1]

3. Gordon says that a "you-message" is a statement of blaming, shaming, warning, or ordering. Its hallmark is that it con-

tains the word "you" (you stop that; you should know better; if you don't stop that, then . . .). By contrast, an "I-message" describes how I feel when such and such is happening (I cannot rest when someone is playing loud music; I get scared and worried that something awful has happened when it's after curfew and you're not in).

4. Tell three "you" messages you recently sent to your adolescents.

5. Identify the primary emotion behind each. (Was it fear or frustration?)

6. Restate each "you" message as an "I" message.

7. At what level of the anger ladder do you and your adolescents usually express anger?

> Summarize discussion and give assignment for the next session: read chapter 8 and do this week's challenge.

8

Good Housekeeping or Groady to the Max?

Goals

- To distinguish between major and minor issues and learn how to deal effectively with each type
- To identify what things are temporary and not majors
- To identify what things are major, nonnegotiable issues

Getting Started

Many of the changes that appear in adolescents are merely cosmetic, temporary, or cultural. Parents would do well to distinguish these minor matters from major value shifts. One youth pastor said, "If you can wash it out, grow it out, or cut it off, don't sweat it!" We spend so much time worrying about the surfaces of our children. We also need to identify the things that are major issues and then we need to major on the majors and minor on the minors.

Group Discussion

1. Think of a time when you were a teenager and you had a major argument over a minor matter with your own parents. What, in your opinion, are some criteria for distinguishing a major area from a minor one?

2. What are the dangers of majoring on the minors?

3. How can giving adolescents more latitude in the minor areas help them begin to achieve the goals of adolescence we

talked about in chapter 1 (see page 34 to review adolescent goals).

4. What was the "norm" for your teen years?

5. What is the current teen "norm"?

6. What is the adult "norm"? What are the areas of conflict between teen standards and adult ones?

7. How much of today's dress and music is cultural?

8. Where is the line between questions of culture and questions of morality?

9. How can you reduce friction in the minor areas of tension with your adolescents?

Summarize discussion and give assignment for the next session: read chapter 9 and do this week's challenge.

9

Majoring on the Majors

Goals

- To define your own key moral values—the ones you hope to instill in your adolescents
- To deal with problem situations when adolescents violate those values

Getting Started

Most parents have an idea of the positive qualities and behaviors they hope their adolescents will choose to value and enact. Take that a step further: consider what your cherished values are and keep them clearly in mind. You will be better able to communicate these values to your kids and to deal with infractions of these values should they occur. For instance, your teens should know how seriously you take the issue of drugs and what you will do to prevent your teens from experimenting with drugs. Other values may be more ambiguous, and you hope your children will internalize these values for themselves. It helps to major on the majors!

Group Discussion

1. What are some of the most important moral values, behaviors, and beliefs you have tried to instill in your adolescents and hope they will choose to claim?

> The group's list of virtues, behaviors, and values might include the following: truthfulness, a forgiving spirit, kindness, sexual purity, self-acceptance, a good work ethic, a personal faith in God, courage, independence, self-control.

2. What are the top five things that are most important to you?

3. For each value or virtue, describe behavior on a continuum. At the far left of the continuum is positive behavior that exemplifies the virtue. At the far right is negative behavior. A continuum for truthfulness, for example, might have these categories:

Tells truth even at cost to self
Tells truth if no cost to self
Tells occasional white lies
Tells lies
Cannot be depended on to tell truth

4. Now define the limits of behavior you consider acceptable in your adolescents. Realize that to some parents, everything is a major. You can only major on so many things so, for this exercise, stick with your top five!

5. Ask these two questions to help determine which issues are major:

Is it a moral issue?
What difference will it make in light of eternity?

6. When adolescents don't cooperate in the major areas, when is it appropriate to get outside help—to pursue counseling, talk to teachers, pastors, and so on?

> Summarize discussion and give assignment for the next session: read chapter 10 and do this week's challenge.

10

Internalizing Values and Making Wise Decisions

Goals

- To help adolescents learn the decision-making process
- To gain an understanding of some techniques of encouraging spiritual growth in your adolescents

Getting Started

Modeling is probably the most effective way to pass on spiritual truths to your adolescents. Remember that God loves both you and your children, and he has your best interest at heart. Your honest mistakes will not ruin your children, but your wrong attitudes can have a negative effect. Nothing stretches a parent's faith quite like having adolescents. Letting them learn decision making by letting go in some areas is scary—even with the Birthday Boxes! When you are tempted to nag, pray instead!

Group Discussion

1. How can you teach your adolescents to make wise decisions?

2. How do you feel about letting your kids make wrong decisions?

3. How can you relax while parenting adolescents?

4. Share your experience, using any of the methods listed below, for how to help your adolescents internalize their own convictions:

- Encourage questions.
- Provide books and tapes.
- Model your faith.
- Discuss steps for negotiating.
- State the problem.
- List possible options.
- Choose a plan of action.
- Try it out. If it doesn't work, choose another and try it.
- Learn to make a pros-and-cons list.

Summarize discussion and give assignment for the next session: read chapter 11 and do this week's challenge.

11

Adolescent Girls and Boys— Understanding the Difference

Goals

- To understand the difference between adolescent girls and adolescent boys
- To learn strategies for relating to each gender

Getting Started

As children reach adolescence, it's important to understand how boys and girls are different. Research documents these differences, which become more pronounced at this stage of development. You will benefit from looking at gender through an adolescent filter and coming up with your own strategy for relating with your sons and daughters during this often turbulent time.

Group Discussion

1. What changes in your kids did you encounter as they reached puberty?

2. Describe your relationship with your children of your own gender and of the other gender. How is your relationship with each different?

3. Do you tend to treat the sexes differently? Place a B for boy or a G for girl before the following statements:

_____ I encourage my adolescents to share feelings.
_____ I am very protective.

_____ I readily give freedom and responsibility.
_____ I hug my child often.
_____ I expect more academically.
_____ I expect more athletically.
_____ I emphasize appearance and grooming.

4. Review and discuss tips for relating to adolescent boys on pages 152–54.

5. Review and discuss tips for relating to adolescent girls on pages 154–56.

6. What could you do today to build a better relationship with your adolescents next week? Next month?

> Summarize discussion.
> Give the assignment for next session: read chapter 12 and do this week's challenge.

12

Midcourse Correction

Goals

- To rebuild trust with your adolescent when he or she blows it
- To learn to trust God when things are difficult

Getting Started

Trust is such a delicate commodity. Like an Alpine flower, it can be easily damaged and take a long time to grow again. But the good news is that it *can* grow again. Through God's help and healing, trust that has been hurt can be healed and restored. Character is sometimes built through failure. Trust is not a one-time gift; it is a gift that must be given over and over again. True parental trust allows some adolescent freedom.

Group Discussion

1. Do you remember breaking trust with your parent? How was the trust reestablished?

2. Share a time that you experienced a trust breakdown with your adolescents. How did you rebuild trust?

3. Review principles from chapter 12 for rebuilding trust, such as

offering new opportunities for building trust
getting all the facts before making a judgment
resisting attacking
being willing to forgive

Which one of these principles seems most difficult to you? Why?

4. How does trusting in God help you to reinvest trust in your adolescents?

5. Review the "trust-busters" (pages 164–66). Which ones are you guilty of?

6. Review tips for dealing with resistant teens. Which ones relate to your present situation?

7. On a scale of 1 to 10, with 10 being complete trust, how would you rank your present level of trust in God?

8. Can you point to any event—recent or long ago—that shook your trust in God? Where you felt he had let you down?

9. How can you reestablish, or grow, in your trust in God?

10. Are you willing to release your children to God's care?

Summarize discussion and give assignment for the next session: read chapter 13 and do this week's challenge. Encourage parents to begin a prayer journal for their children.

13

Relax! Who Me?

Goals

- To relax while parenting adolescents
- To plan for the future

Getting Started

As you learn to release your children to God's ultimate care, and as your adolescents grow in independence, you need to find new areas of personal growth. As your adolescents move toward adulthood, there are still times for advising, but more often you will need to let go. During the active teen years, you can easily lose sight of life outside of parenting. Physical activity can also help overcome the emotional stress of parenting teens. Looking for the humor in each difficult or irritating situation will help you relax. Keep the relationship strong; it's your link for the future!

Group Discussion

1. Can you think of a time you were the "interference runner" with your teenagers and another person, perhaps even the other parent? When have you felt like a "life shaper"?

2. What can you do to "lighten up"?

3. What do you look forward to when your children leave the nest?

4. What personal interests do you have? Which ones would you like to develop?

5. What can you do today to live a more balanced life?

6. If you are married, your most important relationship, apart from the Lord, should be the relationship with your spouse. What can you do to revitalize your marriage? (See our book *10 Great Dates to Revitalize Your Marriage* for some ideas.)

7. Late nights are as much a part of caring for a teenager as caring for a baby. How can you insure you get enough sleep and rest?

8. Proverbs 17:22 says, "A cheerful heart is good medicine." What can you do to develop your sense of humor?

9. Would you like to continue to get together for support and encouragement? How often? Where?

Review the previous discussions and deal with any questions.

Determine if the group will continue to meet together for support and encouragement.

Have a time for sharing what the group has meant to the parents. Lead (or choose someone else to lead) in prayer, thanking God for his love and protection for your adolescents. You may want to close with the verse "Now faith is being sure of what we hope for and certain of what we do not see" (Heb. 11:1).

Certificate of Teenagehood

This is to certify that_____
has successfully completed all tests to prove he is
prepared to enter the wonderful and challenging
world of a teenager.

City_____

Officially Certified This Day

Of_____

"Trust in the LORD with all your heart,
And lean not on your own understanding;
In all your ways acknowledge him
And he will make your paths straight."

Proverbs 3:5–6

Teenage Challenge Completed

SPIRITUAL:

PHYSICAL:

MENTAL:

PRACTICAL:

Parents' signatures

_____

_____

Teen's signature

_____

Anger Ladder

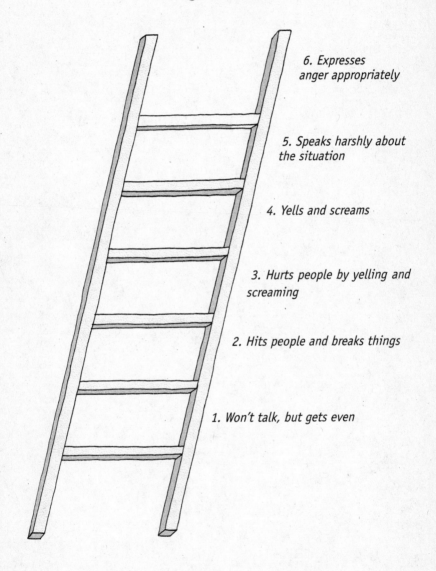

6. *Expresses anger appropriately*

5. *Speaks harshly about the situation*

4. *Yells and screams*

3. *Hurts people by yelling and screaming*

2. *Hits people and breaks things*

1. *Won't talk, but gets even*

NOTES

CHAPTER 1: Will the Well-Rounded Teenager Please Stand Up?

1. Since we did this study on our own adolescents, much temperament research has been done. For a current popular approach, see *Discovering Your Child's Design* by Thom Black. For a more academic approach refer to the research of Thomas and Chess that conceptualizes nine categories of behavioral style: rhythmicity, activity level, attention span-persistence, distractibility, adaptability, approach-withdrawal, threshold, intensity of reaction, and mood.

2. Dave and Claudia Arp, PEP Groups for Parents of Teens, *Building Positive Relationships for the Teen Years* (Elgin, Ill.: David C. Cook, 1994), 20.

3. Merton Strommen and Irene Strommen, *Five Cries of Parents* (New York: Harper & Row, 1985), 6.

4. To further study parenting styles, please refer to the research of Holmbeck, Paikoff, and Brooks-Gunn and Marc H. Bornstein.

5. Style is the environmental or emotional climate, while parenting practices get into more specifics. Holmbeck, Paikoff, and Brooks-Gunn in their chapter "Parenting Adolescents," in *Handbook of Parenting: Applied and Practical Parenting,* Marc H. Bornstein ed. (New Jersey: Lawrence Erlbaum Associates, 1995), 104, summarize the literature, saying, "Adolescents demonstrate more favorable outcomes when parents: (1) set clear standards for their child's behavior; (2) enforce rules and regulations with sanctions that are not overly punitive or facilitative of coercive cycles; (3) provide consistent discipline; (4) explain their assertions; (5) permit give-and-take between parent and child during family discussions; (6) remain involved in the adolescent's daily life and monitor their child's whereabouts without being overprotective; (7) provide a warm, responsive, and cohesive family environment; (8) provide information to the adolescent and aid the adolescent in developing useful skills, particularly in areas where risks are likely; (9) encourage differentiation by allowing adolescents to develop their own opinions within a connected environment."

6. Ibid., 33.

CHAPTER 3: Bird Legs, Braces, and Zits

1. Jay Kesler, *Parents and Teenagers* (Wheaton, Ill.: Victor Books, 1984), 157.
2. Charles Swindoll, *Home, Where Life Makes Up Its Mind* (Portland, Ore.: Multnomah Press, 1980), 51.
3. From John Gottman, *Why Marriages Succeed or Fail* (New York: Simon and Schuster, 1994), 29.
4. Kesler, 285.

CHAPTER 5: The Birthday Box

1. Adapted from Dave and Claudia Arp, PEP Groups for Parents of Teens, Study Book, *Building Positive Relationships for the Teen Years* (Elgin, Ill.: David C. Cook, 1994), 71.

CHAPTER 6: Getting Off the Lecture Circuit

1. Merton Strommen and Irene Strommen, *Five Cries of Parents* (New York: Harper & Row, 1985), 75.

CHAPTER 7: When the Bridge Is Out

1. Haim Ginott, *Between Parent and Teenager* (New York: Macmillan, 1969), 89.
2. Adapted from Dr. Ross Campbell, *How to Really Love Your Teenager* (Wheaton, Ill.: Victor Books, 1981), 66–69.
3. Ibid., 76.

CHAPTER 9: Majoring on the Majors

1. Merton Strommen and Irene Strommen, *Five Cries of Parents* (New York: Harper & Row, 1985), 75.
2. Bruce Narramore, *Adolescence Is Not an Illness* (Old Tappan, N.J.: Revell, 1980), 32.
3. Art Linkletter and George Gallup, Jr., *My Child on Drugs? Youth and the Drug Culture* (Cincinnati, Ohio: Standard Publishing Company, 1981), 15.
4. Ibid.
5. "The Chemistry of Craving," *Psychology Today* (October 1983), 37–38.
6. Linkletter and Gallup, 84–85.
7. Adapted from Jay Kesler, *Parents and Teenagers* (Wheaton, Ill.: Victor Books, 1984).

CHAPTER 10: Internalizing Values and Making Wise Decisions

1. Bruce Narramore, *Adolescence Is Not an Illness* (Old Tappan, N.J.: Revell, 1980), 66–67.
2. Susan Schaeffer Macaulay, *How to Be Your Own Selfish Pig* (Elgin, Ill.: Chariot Books, 1982), 17.

CHAPTER 11: Adolescent Girls and Boys— Understanding the Difference

1. Mary Pipher, *Reviving Ophelia* (New York: Ballantine Books, 1995), 23–24.
2. Ibid., 73.
3. Ibid., 83.
4. "Some Battles with Adolescents Not Worth Waging War," Dr. James Dobson, *Knoxville News-Sentinel,* (Saturday, October 31, 1998), B4.

CHAPTER 12: Midcourse Correction

1. Fritz Ridenour, *What Teenagers Wish Their Parents Knew About Kids* (Waco, Tex.: Word Publishers, 1982), 172.
2. Jay Kesler, *Parents and Teenagers* (Wheaton, III: Victor Books, 1984), 157.
3. Merton Strommen and Irene Strommen, *Five Cries of Parents,* (New York: Harper & Row, 1985), 97–98.
4. Ridenour, *What Teenagers Wish Their Parents Knew About Kids,* 178.

Discussion Guide

1. Dr. Thomas Gordon, *Parent Effectiveness Training* (New York: Plume Books, 1970), 115, 123.

TEN FUN-FILLED COUPLES' NIGHTS OUT®
THAT WILL ENERGIZE YOUR MARRIAGE!

10 Great Dates to Revitalize Your Marriage
David and Claudia Arp
SOFTCOVER 0-310-21091-7

Dating doesn't have to be only a memory or just another boring evening at the movies. David and Claudia Arp have revolutionized dating by creating Couples' Night Out®—memory-making evenings built on key, marriage-enriching themes. This approach to relationship growth involves both partners, is low-key, and best of all, is exciting, proven and FUN!

Draw upon the best tips from David and Claudia Arp's popular marriage Alive Seminars in this book, *10 Great Dates*. You'll learn how to:

- Communicate better
- Build a creative sex life
- Process anger and resolve conflicts
- Develop spiritual intimacy
- Balance busy lifestyles
- And more!

ALSO LOOK FOR...

10 Great Dates to Revitalize Your Marriage Video Curriculum
ISBN 0-310-21350-9

This video curriculum is based on the Marriage Alive Seminars and the *10 Great Dates to Revitalize Your Marriage* book.

The curriculum kit contains:

- two 75-minute videos with ten short date launches
- one *10 Great Dates to Revitalize Your Marriage* softcover (208 pages)
- one Leader's Guide (48 pages)

SEMINARS FOR BUILDING BETTER RELATIONSHIPS

Suddenly They're 13

In this lively seminar, the Arps share the secrets for surviving the adolescent years. Learn how to regroup, release, relate, and relax! You can foster positive family dynamics, add fun and focus to your family and build supportive relationships with other parents. This seminar will help you prepare for the teenage years and then actually enjoy them. It's a great way to launch a PEP Groups for Parents of Teens group.

Marriage Alive

The Arps' most requested seminar is an exciting, fun-filled approach to building thriving marriages. Some of the topics included in this six-hour seminar are prioritizing your marriage, finding unity in diversity, communicating your feelings, processing anger and resolving conflict, cultivating spiritual intimacy, and having an intentional marriage.

The Second Half of Marriage

After the adolescent years comes the empty nest. Let the Arps help you prepare for it. Based on their national survey of long-term marriages and their Gold Medallion Award-winning book, *The Second Half of Marriage*, the Arps reveal eight challenges that all long-term marriages face and give practical strategies for surmounting each. Topics include choosing a partner-focused marriage, renewing the couple friendship, focusing on the future, and growing together spiritually.

For more information about Marriage Alive resources or to schedule the Arps for a Marriage Alive Seminar or other speaking engagement contact:

Marriage Alive International
51 West Ranch Trail
Denver, CO 80465
Phone: (888) 690-6667
Email: mace@marriagealive.org
Website: www.marriagealive.com

About the Authors

Claudia Arp and David Arp, MSSW, a husband-wife team, are founders of Marriage Alive International, a ground-breaking ministry dedicated to providing resources and training to empower congregations to help build better marriages and families. Their Marriage Alive seminar is popular across the U.S. and in Europe.

The Arps are well-known conference speakers, columnists, and authors of numerous books and video curricula including *10 Great Dates* and the Gold Medallion Award-winning *The Second Half of Marriage*. Frequent contributors to print and broadcast media, Dave and Claudia have appeared as empty nest experts on the NBC *Today Show*, CBS *This Morning* and Focus on the Family. Their radio program, *The Family Workshop*, is heard daily on over 200 stations. David and Claudia have been married for over 35 years and have 3 married sons and 7 grandchildren. Visit their website at www.marriagealive.org

---

About Marriage Alive International, Inc.
Bringing marriages and families to life!

Marriage Alive, a church and community-focused ministry, provides easy-to-use, practical marriage and parenting educational resources including video packages, books, and Bible studies. Seminars, consulting, and training are also available. For more information about Marriage Alive resources contact:

Marriage Alive International
51 West Ranch Trail
Denver, CO 80465
Phone: (888) 690-6667
Email: mace@marriagealive.org
Website: www.marriagealive.com